I0410777

S. Hrg. 114–197

THE FIGHT AGAINST ISIS: BUILDING THE COALITION AND ENSURING MILITARY EFFECTIVENESS

HEARING

BEFORE THE

COMMITTEE ON FOREIGN RELATIONS UNITED STATES SENATE

ONE HUNDRED FOURTEENTH CONGRESS

FIRST SESSION

FEBRUARY 25, 2015

Printed for the use of the Committee on Foreign Relations

Available via the World Wide Web: http://www.gpo.gov/fdsys/

U.S. GOVERNMENT PUBLISHING OFFICE

99–368 PDF   WASHINGTON : 2016

For sale by the Superintendent of Documents, U.S. Government Publishing Office
Internet: bookstore.gpo.gov   Phone: toll free (866) 512–1800; DC area (202) 512–1800
Fax: (202) 512–2104   Mail: Stop IDCC, Washington, DC 20402–0001

COMMITTEE ON FOREIGN RELATIONS

BOB CORKER, TENNESSEE, *Chairman*

JAMES E. RISCH, Idaho
MARCO RUBIO, Florida
RON JOHNSON, Wisconsin
JEFF FLAKE, Arizona
CORY GARDNER, Colorado
DAVID PERDUE, Georgia
JOHNNY ISAKSON, Georgia
RAND PAUL, Kentucky
JOHN BARRASSO, Wyoming

ROBERT MENENDEZ, New Jersey
BARBARA BOXER, California
BENJAMIN L. CARDIN, Maryland
JEANNE SHAHEEN, New Hampshire
CHRISTOPHER A. COONS, Delaware
TOM UDALL, New Mexico
CHRISTOPHER MURPHY, Connecticut
TIM KAINE, Virginia
EDWARD J. MARKEY, Massachusetts

LESTER E. MUNSON III, *Staff Director*
JODI B. HERMAN, *Democratic Staff Director*

(II)

CONTENTS

(III)

THE FIGHT AGAINST ISIS: BUILDING THE COALITION AND ENSURING MILITARY EFFECTIVENESS

WEDNESDAY, FEBRUARY 25, 2015

U.S. SENATE,
COMMITTEE ON FOREIGN RELATIONS,
Washington, DC.

The subcommittee met, pursuant to notice, at 1:31 p.m., in room SD–419, Senate Office Building, Hon. Bob Corker (chairman of the committee) presiding.

Present: Senators Corker, Rubio, Johnson, Flake, Gardner, Perdue, Isakson, Paul, Barrasso, Menendez, Boxer, Cardin, Shaheen, Murphy, Kaine, and Markey.

OPENING STATEMENT OF HON. BOB CORKER, U.S. SENATOR FROM TENNESSEE

The CHAIRMAN. I call this meeting of the Foreign Relations Committee to order, and I want to thank General Allen for being here. I know he has a hard stop today at 3:30, and that he has meetings with CENTCOM later that he is traveling to. But I want to thank him for being here, and I will properly introduce him in just a moment.

The President has sent forward a request for the authorization for the use of military force. Because of the nature and the way that this happened in that the conflict has been ongoing for about 6 months now, I think one of the things that most people here are concerned about is that there is a level of confidence in what we are doing, and that it is going to achieve the stated goals that the President has laid out. And I do not know of anybody more equipped to come before us today than General Allen, who has served our country with great distinction.

I think many people feel decently well about what is happening in Iraq. I think there are a lot of questions relative to Syria. My sense is today you will have a number of questions regarding that. And we hope that what you will do, General Allen, is give us an honest assessment as to the end state that we would like to see happen in Iraq and Syria when we complete the activities that we are involved in, and understand the political and military strategy that we have underway, and to give us a little sense of timeframe relative to the various activities that are necessary.

I was just in Iraq last week in both Baghdad and Erbil with our Kurdish friends, and then over in Ankara with our Turkish friends, and I will say that the Shia militias are everywhere in Iraq, as people know. General Suleimani, who is head of the Quds Force for Iran, has now become a celebrity in Iraq. And I have to say it feels very strange to be there knowing that much of the activity that we have underway, while it is necessary, is really to Iran's benefit. And I know there are a lot of concerns that after this activity is completed if we are successful with ISIS, which I know we will be, in essence, the next issue is going to be dealing with security of forces there with the Shia militias.

I was happy to see that Turkey has gone ahead and signed an agreement, train and equip agreement. I am sure that is something that you have made happen, and thank you for that. At the same time, I know there are a lot of concerns right now about how we deal with Assad's barrel bombs as we train and equip these individuals. How do we protect them from the barrel bombs, which cause them to diminish in a greater number than they can be trained? And I am sure that you are going to talk about that.

There is a lot of discussion, as you know, on the ground there about an air exclusion zone—I know you will have some questions about that—and just no-fly discussions. It may be taking place to draw Turkey more into what is happening in Syria itself, which I think most of it—most of us believe is very important.

So as we—as I close, I just want to say we owe it to our nation as we consider this to know that the full range of America's elements of national power, diplomatic, economic, and military means are aligned in such a way to get to the administration's stated goals. Because of the nature of this decision, one, again, this being made after the fact, all of us need to have confidence that the administration is truly committed to achieving the stated goals that they have laid out. And I think your testimony here is going to be very valuable to us.

And with that, I would like to turn to our distinguished ranking member, Senator Menendez, who has been a great partner on all of these issues.

STATEMENT OF HON. BOB MENENDEZ, U.S. SENATOR FROM NEW JERSEY

Senator MENENDEZ. Well, thank you, Mr. Chairman. Thank you for calling the hearing for our work forward on this. And, General Allen, welcome back to the committee, and thank you for your distinguished service to our country in so many different ways, including your present position as a special envoy.

Although this hearing is not focused on the administration's proposed authorization for the use of military force against ISIL, it is by nature an opportunity to probe the dynamics of our current anti-ISIL strategy that will inform our discussion of an AUMF, and specifically whether a strategy that relies on U.S. air power and logistics, intelligence, and training support, but not on U.S. troops on the ground, would be successful in achieving our ultimate goal to end the barbaric rampage of ISIL.

There are those who believe that it is up to our local partners on the ground to ultimately take this war across the finish line. I have heard from others who believe that ISIL cannot be defeated without a significant U.S. ground commitment. So I would like to hear from you, General Allen, where you come down on what will be required to eradicate ISIL, given that we hear reports from Secretary Carter's meetings in Kuwait that while the anti-ISIL strategy does not require fundamental recalibration, our coalition partners can be doing more.

My view personally is that the United States must help combat ISIL and restore stability to the region, and we must follow through on our commitments to our Arab partners. But large-scale U.S. ground forces at this time in this complex political and military atmosphere would at the end of the day decisively increase the prospect of losing a long war.

Now, I appreciate and want to salute all the men and women who are waging a campaign against ISIL, particularly from the air, all of the airstrikes that have, according to your own testimony, inflicted significant damage. And those are promising, and we salute the men and women who do that. But our effectiveness in combating this threat I think cannot be measured only in the number of sorties flown or bombs dropped.

So today's hearing is a welcome opportunity to step back and assess the big picture, the state of the coalition, what will it ultimately take to defeat ISIL, and what we know, I think, will be a multiyear effort that will take billions of dollars, significant military assets, and the painstaking patience of diplomacy matched to all of those efforts.

We look forward to your insights, and we welcome you back to the committee.

The CHAIRMAN. Our distinguished witness today is Gen. John Allen, the Special Presidential Envoy for the Global Coalition to Counter ISIS. General Allen is a retired U.S. Marine four-star general, former commander of ISAF and U.S. forces in Afghanistan. Upon his retirement from the Marine Corps, he was appointed as the senior advisor to the Secretary of Defense on Middle East security. He is currently on a leave of absence from Brookings Institution, where he is codirector of the 21st Century Security and Intelligence Center.

We thank you for your frankness. We thank you for your service to our country. We thank you for being here today. I know you are going to have an unusually long opening comment, which we appreciate, and then we will turn to questions.

STATEMENT OF GEN. JOHN R. ALLEN, USMC (RETIRED), SPECIAL PRESIDENTIAL ENVOY FOR THE GLOBAL COALITION TO COUNTER ISIL, U.S. DEPARTMENT OF STATE, WASHINGTON, DC

General ALLEN. Chairman Corker, thank you, and Ranking Member Menendez, it is good to be back today. Esteemed members of the committee, I want to thank you for providing me the opportunity to update you on the progress of the Global Coalition to Counter ISIL. And let me just add as well my deep and sincere thanks for all that this committee has done for our Department of State, for our diplomats, and for the members of the Department who are serving with such great courage and capability at the far-flung locations of American influence. This committee has done marvelous work to support them, and I want to thank you very much for that.

I just returned to Washington yesterday afternoon from Kuwait where, at the request of Secretary of Defense Ashton Carter, I joined a group of more than 30 senior U.S. diplomats and military commanders for a wide-ranging discussion on our counter-ISIL strategy. While my role as senior special presidential envoy is concerned with the consolidation and the integration of the coalition contributions, not the coordination of its military activities, I remain nonetheless closely synced with my colleagues in the military, and we meet regularly with other departments and agencies involved to review the progress of the counter-ISIL activities.

In addition, we are also discussing the coalition's next step now that we have largely achieved the objectives of the campaign's first phase, which was to blunt ISIL's strategic operational and tactical momentum in Iraq. Through over 2,500 coordinated coalition airstrikes in support of our partners on the ground, we have degraded ISIL's leadership, its logistical and operational capabilities, and we are denying it essential sanctuary in Iraq from which it can plan and execute attacks.

With New Zealand's very welcome announcement yesterday that it will provide military trainers to build the capacity of the Iraqi Security Forces, a dozen coalition nations now participating in these efforts are operating from multiple sites across Iraq. Still the situation in Iraq remains complex, and the road ahead will be challenging and nonlinear. Considering where we were only 8 months ago, one can begin to see how the first phase of the strategy is delivering results.

As I appear before this esteemed committee today, it is important to recall that in June of last year, ISIL burst into the international scene as a seemingly irresistible force. It conquered a city, Mosul, of 1.5 million, then poured south down the Tigris River Valley toward Baghdad, taking cities, and town, and villages along the way. Outside Tikrit, it rounded up and massacred over 1,000 Iraqi army recruits, and to the west it broke through the border town of Al-Qaim and poured east toward Baghdad. ISIL's spokesman, Abu Mohammad al-Adnani, vowed, ''The battle will soon rage in Baghdad and in the holy city of Karbala.''

Shortly thereafter, ISIL launched a multiple-pronged attack further into northern Iraq, massacring minority populations, enslaving hundreds of women and girls, surrounding tens of thousands of Yazidis on Sinjar Mountain, and opening clear route to Erbil, the region's capital.

Then the United States acted. Since our first airstrikes in August, ISIL's advance has been blunted, and they have been driven back from the approaches to Baghdad and Erbil. ISIL lost half of its Iraq-based leadership, thousands of hardened fighters, and is no longer able to amass and maneuver effectively, and to communicate as an effective force. Iraqis are also standing on their feet. The Kurdish peshmerga have recovered nearly all of the ground lost in August, and the peshmerga have also taken control of the Mosul Dam, the Rabiya Crossing with Syria, the Sinjar Mountain, Zumar, and the Kisik Road junction, which eliminated a supply route for ISIL from Syria to Mosul. These forces also broke the siege of the Bayji oil refinery and have begun to push north into the Tigris Valley.

To the west, Sunni tribes are working with Iraq Security Forces to retake the land in the heart of Al-Anbar, a land I know well. And just last week under the cover of bad weather, ISIL launched an attack on the town of al-Baghdadi near the Al-Asad Airbase in Al-Anbar, where our forces are located with the Danes and the Australians to help to train Iraqi soldiers and tribal volunteers.

ISIL, as it has done over and over again, rampaged through the town, killing civilians and driving hundreds of families into the safe haven of the airbase. But the Iraqis did not sit idle. They organized and fought back. Prime Minister Abadi went to the Joint Operations Center in Baghdad and ordered an immediate counter attack. The Minister of Defense flew to Al-Asad to organize available forces, and Iraq army commanders sent an armored column from Baghdad to road march to al-Baghdadi to join the attack. And Sunni tribal volunteers organized to support and, in some cases, led the attack.

Today, much of al-Baghdadi is back in the hands of these local and tribal forces. And I was at Al-Asad just last month, and my deputy, Brett McGurk, was there just 3 days ago, I would tell you that all Americans would be proud to see what our troops are doing there, helping the Iraqis and the tribes to join the battle against ISIL. But this is only the start, and ISIL remains a substantial foe.

But any aura of the invincibility of ISIL has been shattered. ISIL is not invincible. It is defeatable, and it is being defeated by Iraqi Forces defending and taking back their towns, and their cities, and ultimately their country with the support of the United States and the coalition. And importantly, very importantly, the aura of the so-called caliphate is destroyed, and the future of the so-called Caliph Abu Bakr Baghdadi is very much in doubt.

Because we lack the same kind of partners on the ground in Syria, the situation there is more challenging and more complex. Still, we are working closely with regional partners to establish sites for training and equipping vetted and moderate Syrian opposition elements to train approximately 5,000 troops per year for the next 3 years. These and other military aspects of the campaign will inevitably receive the most attention, but as I have seen in the four previous coalition efforts in which I have been involved, it will ultimately be the aggregate pressure of the campaign activity over multiple, mutually supporting lines of effort that will determine the campaign's success.

This is why when I visit a coalition capital and when I meet with a Prime Minister, or a King, or a President, I describe the coalition's counter-ISIL strategy as being organized around multiple lines of effort: the military line to deny safe haven and provide security assistance, disrupting the flow of foreign fighters, disrupting ISIL's financial resources, providing humanitarian relief and support to its victims, and counter messaging or defeating the idea of ISIL.

Since mid-September I have traveled to 21 partner capitals, several of them multiple times, to meet with national leadership there. And in that short span we have assembled a global coalition of 62 nations and international organizations. Of the many recent visits, leaders have expressed heightened concern for the immediate and generational challenge presented by foreign fighters, and rightly so.

Through capacity building in the Balkans, criminal justice efforts in North Africa, and changes to laws in more than a dozen countries, partners are working together to make it more difficult for citizens to fight in Syria and Iraq.

Even with these expanded measures, foreign fighters continue to make their way to the battlefield. We must continue to harmonize our border and customs processes and promote intelligence sharing among our partners. This kind of information-sharing has allowed the coalition to make significant gains on synchronizing practices to block ISIL's access to banks within the region and globally. This includes stemming the flow of private donations and restricting ISIL's ability to generate oil revenues. We are now expanding these efforts to counter ISIL's access to local and informal financial networks.

The coalition is also supporting the United Nations' efforts to provide food and aid and supply critical assistance to protect the vulnerable children, and women, and men from harsh winter conditions in the region. The ravaged communities ISIL leaves in its wake bear witness to ISIL's true identity, one we are actively working with coalition partners to expose with Arab partners taking a leading role.

ISIL was attractive to many of its recruits because of its proclamation of the so-called caliphate and the sense of inevitability that it promoted. The last 6 months have amply demonstrated that ISIL is really operating as a criminal gang and a death cult, which is under increasing pressure as it sends naive and gullible recruits to die by the hundreds.

Coalition partners are working together as never before to share messages, engage traditional and social media, and underscore the vision of religious leaders who reject ISIL's millennialist vision. As the President announced recently, we are partnering with the United Arab Emirates to create a joint messaging center that will contest ISIL's vigorous information offensive and extremist messages for the long term. And we are seeking to create a network of these centers, a global network where a regional consortia of nations can dispute and ultimately dominate the information space filled with ISIL's messaging.

The President has outlined a framework for the authorities he believes will be necessary to pursue this long-term campaign with his formal request to the Congress for the authorization for the use of military force against ISIL. The AUMF request foresees using our unique capabilities in support of partners on the ground instead of through large-scale deployments of U.S. ground forces. The President has asked for flexibility to fight an adaptable enemy, one that hopes to expand his reach beyond the borders of Iraq and Syria.

Taking the fight to ISIL requires that we be flexible and patient in our efforts. It also requires close coordination with this committee and with the Congress so that we are constantly evaluating our tactics and our strategy, and that we are resourcing them appropriately.

Chairman and Ranking Member Menendez, I thank you for the opportunity to be before this committee today and to continue that process of coordination and consultation with you. And I look forward to taking your questions.

[The prepared statement of General Allen follows:]

PREPARED STATEMENT OF GEN. JOHN R. ALLEN

Chairman Corker, Ranking Member Menendez, esteemed members of the committee, thank you for providing me the opportunity to update you on the progress of the Global Coalition to Counter ISIL.

I just returned to Washington late yesterday from Kuwait, where at the request of Secretary of Defense Ashton Carter, I joined a group of more than 30 senior U.S. diplomats and military commanders for a wide ranging discussion of the counter-ISIL strategy and progress to date.

While my role as Special Envoy is concerned with the consolidation and integration of coalition contributions, not the coordination of its military activities, I remain closely synced with my colleagues in the military, and we meet regularly with other departments and agencies involved to review progress of the coalition's counter-ISIL activities.

In addition, we are discussing the coalition's next steps now that we have largely achieved the objective for the campaign's first phase: to blunt ISIL's strategic, operational, and tactical momentum in Iraq.

Through over 2,500 coordinated coalition airstrikes in support of our partners on the ground, we have degraded ISIL's leadership, logistical, and operational capability, and are denying it a sanctuary in Iraq from which it can plan and execute attacks.

With New Zealand's announcement yesterday that it will provide military trainers to build the capacity of Iraqi Security Forces, a dozen coalition nations are now participating in these efforts in multiple sites across Iraq.

Still, the situation in Iraq remains extraordinarily complex, and the road ahead will be challenging and nonlinear. But considering where we were only 8 months ago, one begins to see how this first phase of our strategy is delivering results.

In June of last year, ISIL burst into the international scene as a genocidal and seemingly unstoppable juggernaut. It conquered a city, Mosul, of 1.5 million, then poured south toward Baghdad, taking cities, towns, and villages along the way. Outside Tikrit, it rounded up and massacred over 1,000 Iraqi Air Force recruits. To the west, it broke through the border town of Al-Qaim, and poured east toward Baghdad. ISIL's spokesman, Abu Mohammed al-Adnani, vowed: "The battle would soon rage in Baghdad and [in the holy city of] Karbala." Shortly thereafter, ISIL launched a multiple pronged attack further into northern Iraq, massacring minority populations, enslaving hundreds of women and girls, surrounding tens of thousands of Yazidis at Sinjar mountain, and opening a clear route to Erbil, the region's capital.

Then the United States acted. Since our first airstrikes in August, ISIL's advance has been largely blunted, and has been driven back away from the regional capitals of Baghdad and Erbil. It has also lost half of its Iraq-based leadership and thousands of hardened fighters, and is no longer able to mass, maneuver, and communicate as an effective force.

Iraqis are also standing on their feet. The Kurdish peshmerga have recovered nearly all of the ground lost in August. Peshmerga have taken control of Mosul Dam, Rabiya border crossing, Sinjar Mountain, Zumar, and the Kisik road junction, which eliminated a supply route for ISIL from Syria to Mosul. Iraqi Security Forces with popular volunteers have secured the routes to Baghdad, and the capital is now seeing the lowest levels of violence it's seen in years. These forces also broke the siege of the Bayji oil refinery, and have begun to push north up the Tigris Valley. To the west, Sunni tribes are working with Iraqi Security Forces to retake land in the heart of Anbar province, land I know well.

Just last week, under the cover of bad weather, ISIL launched an attack the town of Al-Baghdadi, near Al-Asad Airbase, where our forces are located with the Danes and Australians to help train Iraqi soldiers and tribal volunteers. ISIL, as it has done over and over again , rampaged through the town, killing civilians, and driving hundreds of families into exile on the airbase. But the Iraqis did not sit idle; they organized, and fought back.

Prime Minister Abadi went to the Joint Operations Center in Baghdad and ordered a counterattack. The Minister of Defense flew to Al-Asad to organize available forces. Iraqi Army commanders sent an armored column from Baghdad to join the attack. Sunni tribal volunteers organized to support and in some cases lead the attack. Today, much of Al-Baghdadi is back in the hands of these local tribes and security forces. I was at Al-Asad Airbase last month, and my deputy, Brett McGurk, was there 3 days ago. All Americans would be proud to see what our troops are doing there, helping the Iraqis and the tribes join the battle against ISIL. This is only a start, and ISIL will remain a formidable foe: but any aura of invincibility has been shattered. ISIL is not invincible, it is defeatable, and is being defeated— by Iraqi forces, defending and taking back their towns, villages, and cities with the support of the United States and the coalition.

Because we lack the same kind of partners on the ground in Syria, the situation is more challenging and complex there. Still, we are working closely with regional partners to establish sites for training and equipping vetted, moderate Syrian opposition elements, to train approximately 5,000 troops per year for the next 3 years. On February 19, we formalized a framework on Turkey's support for the Department of Defense's train and equip activities for the moderate Syrian opposition.

These and other military aspects of the campaign will inevitably receive the most attention. But as I saw in Afghanistan during my command there, in Iraq in Al-Anbar in 2007–08, and in recovery efforts for the 2004 South Asian tsunami, the military effort is essential but not sufficient.

It will ultimately be the aggregate pressure of the coalition's activity over multiple, mutually supporting lines of effort that will determine a campaign's success.

That is why when I visit a coalition capital and meet with a prime minister, a king, or president, I describe the coalition component of the counter-ISIL strategy as being organized around multiple lines of effort including the military line to deny safe haven and provide security assistance, disrupting the flow of foreign fighters, disrupting ISIL's financial resources, providing humanitarian relief and support to its victims, and countermessaging . . . or defeating ISIL as an idea.

Since mid-September, I have traveled to 21 partner capitals, several of them multiple times, to meet with the national leadership. In that short span, we have assembled a global coalition of 62 nations and international organizations.

Among Coalition members, disrupting the flow of foreign fighters is an urgent concern in all of these conversations . . . and rightly so. There is no question that the thousands of young men who have traveled to fight in Syria and Iraq present a truly unprecedented, generational challenge.

Today, coalition members are coming together to take the coordinated actions required to meet this growing threat.

More than a dozen nations have changed laws and penalties to make it more difficult to travel and fight in Syria and Iraq. Through capacity building in the Balkans, criminal justice efforts in North Africa, and a 20 million euro investment from the European Union to engage at-risk communities, governments are taking a series of concerted actions.

Even with these expanded measures, foreign fighters continue to stream to the battlefields of Syria and Iraq . . . so we are enhancing our cooperation with key international partners to confront this threat. We must continue to improve how we harmonize border and customs processes, track potential and actual fighters en route to the battle, and share intelligence with partners.

This kind of information-sharing and creative thinking between partners is also vital in meeting a related and similarly urgent challenge: constraining ISIL's access to financial support.

Here, the coalition has made significant gains in synchronizing practices to block ISIL's access to banks, both in the region and globally. This includes stemming the flow of private donations and limiting ISIL's financial options by restricting its ability to generate oil revenues. We are now expanding these efforts to counter ISIL's access to local and informal financial networks.

As we come together to curb ISIL's financial support, we are also providing urgent assistance to ISIL's victims.

The coalition is supporting the United Nations' efforts to provide food aid and supply critical assistance to protect vulnerable women, children and men from harsh winter conditions. Saudi Arabia alone has contributed $500M in aid in support of the U.N. appeal for Iraq, and has provided more than a dozen medical camps; numerous partners have made substantial investments in education for refugee children and in host communities. The United States alone has contributed close to $4 billion in assistance for many of the 13 million displaced Iraqis and Syrians. But we and our partners must do more.

The communities and refugees left in ISIL's wake bear witness to ISIL's true identity, one we are actively working with coalition partners to expose, with Arab partners taking a leading role.

ISIL is attractive to many of its recruits because it proclaimed the Caliphate, and emerged onto the world stage with self-proclaimed inevitability and invincibility. But the last 6 months have amply demonstrated that ISIL is little more than a criminal gang and death cult, which now finds itself under increasing pressure, sending naive and gullible recruits to die by the hundreds.

Our coalition partners are working together as never before to share messages, engage traditional and social media and underscore the vision of religious leaders and the international community that rejects ISIL's millennialist vision. As the President announced recently, we are partnering with the U.A.E. to create a joint messaging center that will contest ISIL's vigorous offensive in the information battlespace.

In confronting these enduring challenges, the coalition can take some confidence from what it has already helped to achieve. We as a country and as a coalition will inevitably have good days and hard days on the battlefield and we are still in the early stages of a long-term campaign.

The President has outlined a framework for the authorities he believes will be necessary to pursue this long-term campaign with his formal request to Congress for the authorization of the use of military force against ISIL. The AUMF request foresees using our unique capabilities in support of partners on the ground . . . instead of through the use of large-scale deployment of U.S. ground forces. At the same time, the President has asked for the flexibility to fight an adaptable enemy, one that is expanding its reach and capabilities well beyond the borders of Iraq and Syria. Taking the fight to ISIL requires that we be flexible and patient in our efforts. It also requires close coordination with this committee and with Congress, so that we are constantly evaluating our tactics and strategy, and that we are resourcing them appropriately.

This hearing presents an opportunity to continue that process of coordination and consultation. I want to thank you again for the invitation to speak with you and look forward to taking your questions.

The CHAIRMAN. We thank you for the testimony and for your great service to our country.

Yesterday Senator Kerry testified that he felt like that today the administration already has, because of the 2001 AUMF and the 2002 AUMF, the authority to conduct the operations that are being conducted in Iraq and Syria. Do you agree with that assessment?

General ALLEN. I do, Chairman.

The CHAIRMAN. Okay. So it is an interesting place that we find ourselves where 6 months after conflicts have begun, a new AUMF is being offered. And I know that in order to pursue one properly through Congress, it is standard process to submit one, which I appreciate. But it is an interesting place that those authorities already exist.

The train and equip program that you have been able to negotiate, many concerns have been raised about the fact that most of the free Syrian opposition initially was targeting Assad. That was the reason for their being. Now we are organizing these against ISIS, and my understanding is we are going against an entirely different recruitment group to do that. Are we finding that to be an easy recruitment process?

General ALLEN. As we began this, Chairman, we were not sure, frankly, how that recruitment process would unfold. Just 2 days ago I had the opportunity to have a conversation with the great soldier that the United States has put against this challenge, General Nagata. And I will not go into the details of the numbers, but the numbers are much higher than we thought actually. And it has been a very encouraging—we have had an encouraging sense that there is an interest in this—in this outcome.

The CHAIRMAN. So my sense is there are, based on my experiences last week, there are larger groups of people that are willing to go against ISIS initially in this train and equip than some initially thought. Is that correct?

General ALLEN. That is correct, Chairman.

The CHAIRMAN. So let me ask you this question. One of the big moral dilemmas I think is that as we train and equip these folks, we know that Assad is, in fact, barrel bombing other members of the Free Syrian Army today. I know that is a loose description of who it is that is opposing him. But my understanding is there have been significant discussions with Turkey over an air exclusion zone in the northwestern Aleppo area and a no-fly zone along the border. And that has been the issue that has hindered them actually getting more involved in the conflict even though they are working with us more fully than they have in multiple areas, some of which I will not mention here. That has been the issue that has kept them from actually getting more involved.

It is also my understanding that that decision, the decision to do that, is at the President's desk. It is at the White House, and he has not made a decision yet as to whether to engage. Can you update us on that or tell us the effect of that decision not being made on Turkey getting more involved in the conflict, and helping us with those ground operations you were talking about earlier?

General ALLEN. Well, I will start by, you know, reciting what I have said before with respect to Turkey, and it is we have an old friendship with Turkey, and they are an ally. And where we began this conversation just some months and where we are today, I think there has been significant progress in the conversation about Turkey's role in the coalition and all that we want to accomplish together, and, in particular, what we would like to accomplish in Syria.

That conversation is not over, but there has been much progress. I just met with a Turkish delegation yesterday, and I intend to head back to Ankara in the very near future to continue that conversation. And part of that conversation obviously is those measures or those measures that can be taken either collectively or by a larger coalition to provide protection for the moderate Syrian elements that we support and ultimately will produce over time.

And I will not get into the specific details of the negotiation, but that is a very important part of the conversation, and we are going to continue that conversation in the future.

The CHAIRMAN. But it is fair to say that there are some significant decisions that our government needs to make relative to those protections. And if they are made, could break a little bit of a logjam relative to greater involvement by Turkey. That would be a fair assessment. Is that correct?

General ALLEN. It is a fair assessment, Chairman. The details of what the conversation can be can lead us in several different directions. There was the initial conversation about a formal no-fly zone, which was heavily or very specifically and purposefully laid out on a map. The real issue is not necessarily a no-fly zone. It is how do we protect our allies.

The CHAIRMAN. That is right.

General ALLEN. And that is the nature of the conversation. And putting all measures necessary to be able to provide for that protection is the heart of the conversation that we are going to continue to have with the Turks.

The CHAIRMAN. And one final question, and then I will stop and turn it over to Senator Menendez. In the event that we needed to protect those that we are training and equipping and other members of the Free Syrian Army, in the event we needed to protect them against Assad barrel bombing them, do you believe that is something that needs an additional authority other than what is now being requested?

General ALLEN. I would have to study that, Chairman. My hope is that we would be able to provide the kind of protection that they need and they deserve within the authorization that we are currently proposing.

The CHAIRMAN. You would want to make sure that we knew that that type of authorization was a part of anything we may do.

General ALLEN. Oh, I think so, yes, sir. That is going to be clearly a part of the outcome.

The CHAIRMAN. Senator Menendez.

Senator MENENDEZ. Thank you, Mr. Chairman. General Allen, you are a retired U.S. Marine, four-star general. You were the former commander of NATO's International Security Assistance Force and the U.S. Forces in Afghanistan for about a year and a half. And then you became the senior advisor to the Secretary of Defense on Middle East security.

You commanded during that period of time 150,000 U.S. and NATO Forces in Afghanistan during a critical period of the war. And I put that out there, one, in recognition of that service, and, two, in also the framework of my question. What does ''no enduring combat forces'' mean?

General ALLEN. I think obviously the nature of the contingency, or the emergency, or the potential conflict will give us the indications of what kinds of measures would need to be taken in the aggregate to deal with that emergency, to give the President the kinds of options that he needs in order to protect the lives of American citizens and American interests in the homeland.

Each one of these emergencies will be different. Each one will require a different aggregation of American hard and soft power ultimately to solve them. And so, I think it would be difficult to put necessarily a level of precision against the word ''enduring.'' I think what we will seek to do, and I believe this Administration and future administrations would be obviously very interested in consulting with the Congress about each particular emergency.

Senator MENENDEZ. I appreciate a consultation. The problem is you referenced your answer in the context of emergencies, but ''no enduring offensive combat troops'' does not necessarily only apply to emergencies. If you send 20,000 troops there in there for 4 months, is that enduring?

General ALLEN. Again, Senator, I think that trying to put a specific amount of time on the word ''enduring''——

Senator MENENDEZ. So it is neither time nor size.

General ALLEN. I think we take a full appreciation of what we are facing.

Senator MENENDEZ. Okay.

General ALLEN. And I believe that we give the President the options necessary in order to deal with the emergency. And ''enduring'' might only be 2 weeks, but enduring might be 2 years. I think we need to ensure that we put the right resources against the contingency and give us the amount of time necessary, ''us'' being all the American people, the time necessary to solve the problem.

Senator MENENDEZ. And I think you have honestly stated the challenge that we have. Two weeks is one thing, 2 years is another, and this is the problem with the language as it exists. There is no clear defining element of the authorization given to the President in which hundreds, but then maybe tens of thousands of troops could be sent. They could be sent for long periods of time.

That is a challenge. And so, how do we get our arms around that, you know. I think I can fairly speak for Democrats. We want to fight ISIL. We want to give the President the wherewithal to degrade and deter them. But we cannot provide a blank check to this and a future President because everything that is envisioned goes beyond this President. So I wanted to use your expertise to try to put my arms around it, and I see the challenge that we have.

Let me ask you this. Following up on the chairman's questions, is it not basically true that unless we buy into something that is about getting rid of Assad, Turkey is really not going to engage here with us in the way we want them to?

General ALLEN. The Turks have not indicated that to me in our conversations. I think we share the same goal with respect to Syria, and that is the solution to Syria is not going to be determined by military force, that they ultimately desire a political outcome in Syria that is the will of the Syrian people, and that that outcome is one that does not include Bashar al-Assad.

I think we share that goal with Turkey, but I have not had in my conversations with the Turks the requirement that we take concerted action against Bashar al-Assad as the precondition necessarily for the Turks to have any greater role in the coalition to deal with ISIL.

Senator MENENDEZ. Is it not true that Turkey at this point still is allowing foreign fighters to cross its borders into Syria?

General ALLEN. If foreign fighters get across the border from Turkey, it is not because the Turks are allowing them. Again, I had a conversation with them yesterday. I have watched them grip this problem. It is a greater problem than many of us had imagined at the beginning. They have attempted to strengthen their border crossing protocols. We are seeking greater information-sharing and intelligence-sharing with them in that regard. We are restructuring some elements of the coalition specifically to focus the capabilities of nations on the issue of the movement and the dealing of foreign fighters through transit states, of which the Turks are going to play an important role in that process within the coalition.

So do foreign fighters cross Turkey and get into Syria? Yes, they do. Are the Turks permitting them to do that? I do not believe so, and I think that the Turks are working hard ultimately to take the measures necessary to staunch that flow as much as they can.

Senator MENENDEZ. One final question on Iran. Iran is in the midst of Iraq. It is in the midst of Syria. Do we share mutual goals with Iran?

General ALLEN. Well, I would say that our goals with respect to Iraq is that we return Iraq to the sovereign control of the Iraqi people and to the central government in Baghdad.

Senator MENENDEZ. Do you think the Iranians share that view?

General ALLEN. Oh, I believe so. I believe the Iranians would believe that their interests—would consider that their interests are best served by an Iraq——

Senator MENENDEZ. Because they have very significant influence in Iraq.

General ALLEN. Well, they have regional interests, and those interests are, in fact, in Iraq. That is not something that should surprise us or necessarily alarm us.

Senator MENENDEZ. I am looking beyond, so if we think an accommodation to fight ISIL is good, the aftermath of that in Iraq, in Syria, in Yemen, and elsewhere, in my view, is not so good. And so, sometimes we look at the short game versus the long one, and I am concerned about what the long one is.

General ALLEN. Well, Senator, I would not propose that we are accommodating Iran in Iraq at this particular moment. We are undertaking the measures that we taking in Iraq with the Iraqis. We are not cooperating with the Iranians. But as you have pointed out and as your question presupposes, the Iranians have an interest in a stable Iraq, just as we in the region have an interest in a stable Iraq. But that does not mean we are accommodating the Iranians by virtue of the actions that we are taking in Iraq.

Senator MENENDEZ. Thank you.

The CHAIRMAN. Senator Johnson.

Senator JOHNSON. Thank you, Mr. Chairman. General Allen, thank you for your service. I did not envy your task. In your testimony you say that ISIS has lost half of its Iraq-based leadership. How do we know that?

General ALLEN. I am sorry. Say again your question again, sir?

Senator JOHNSON. You said that ISIS has lost half of its Iraq-based leadership. How do we know that? Do we have pretty good intelligence for that?

General ALLEN. We actually do have pretty good intelligence on this matter, and in the process of tracking the elements within the senior echelons of ISIL's leadership, we have been tracking and systematically, as we are able to find them, dealing with them.

Senator JOHNSON. You also said that in the last 6 months we have amply demonstrated that ISIS is ''little more than a criminal gang and death cult, which now finds itself under increasing pressure, sending naive and gullible recruits to die by the hundreds.'' What is your evaluation of the accretion versus degradation ratio? How many people are coming into the battle, actually being drawn and recruited by what they see in ISIS versus the number of people who really are dying?

General ALLEN. Well, I think that is a difficult number to——

Senator JOHNSON. Is it positive or negative? Are more people joining the fight versus what we are able to degrade?

General ALLEN. Well, I would say two things. The numbers are up, and the numbers are up because we are now tracking the numbers in ways we have not before. I think the numbers are also up because of the so-called caliphate, and that has created in some respects a magnetism for those elements that want to be part of this, that want to support this emergence within their own sense of their faith. And so, that has created a recruiting opportunity for ISIL that they had not had before.

So we are going to continue to track those numbers. It is not just a matter of dealing with those numbers in the battle space. We are dealing with those numbers by virtue of taking other measures. As my testimony indicated, we operate along five lines of effort. The military line is only one of them. Another line where I think we will be seeing more traction be realized as time goes on will be the consortium of nations that are taking the necessary steps to make it difficult to be recruited in a country, to transit out of that country, and ultimately get to the battle space.

Plus as ISIL's so-called caliphate, as it continues to receive blow after blow and ultimately be proven as not being inevitable or invincible, using that as an opportunity to truly message what this organization is to decrease its attractiveness to those who might otherwise be attracted and seek to move to the battle space ultimately to support them. It will take all those measures in concert, sir.

Senator JOHNSON. So that kind of leads me to my next question. Defeat sounds good, but can you describe what defeat looks like?

General ALLEN. Is that this organization has been rendered ineffective in its capability of being an existential threat to Iraq. We are not going to eradicate or annihilate ISIL. Most of these organizations that we have dealt with before, there will be some residue of that organization for a long period of time to come. But we do not want it to have operational capabilities that create the opportunity for it to threaten the existence of Iraq or other states in the region.

We want to diminish its capacity to generate funding, which limits dramatically its operational decision making and capabilities to affect discretion with respect to its recruiting and its battlefield capabilities. We want to compete with it and ultimately overcome or defeat its message in the information sphere where it has achieved a significant capability and recruiting prowess.

So across the many different measures of our lines of effort, we have a sense of what we want to do in the physical sphere, how we want to deal with them in the financial sphere, and ultimately how we want to deal with them in the information sphere. And all of those together will constitute the defeat of ISIL.

Senator JOHNSON. You mentioned the establishment of the caliphate. The article in The Atlantic really kind of laid out that that is a draw. That is a pull. That establishes certain benchmarks, a certain motivation for people being recruited. It relies on territorial gains or a hold onto territory. Is that part of defeat, to deny them all territory?

General ALLEN. Absolutely.

Senator JOHNSON. To destroy them so that the caliphate no longer exists? So we are talking about pretty much decimation, correct? That is what Secretary Kerry—that was the word he used, "decimate." You know, a few people scattered maybe around the world—kind of like after Nazi Germany—but pretty well decimated. That is not exactly what I am hearing out of you.

General ALLEN. Well, we can apply whatever term you would like to. "Decimation" is clearly one of the terms that we might apply to it. We want them to have no operational capability in the end, and that means breaking them into small organizations that do not have the capacity as it begins to attempt to mass to be a threat.

Senator JOHNSON. Define a "small organization." Again, I am just trying to get some sense of what we mean by defeat. It sounds great, to deny them operational capabilities. Are we talking about taking 30,000 down to 500? Are we taking 30,000 down to 10,000 broken up into 10 different groups?

General ALLEN. It will take time. It will take time that will ultimately be realized in a number of ways. It will be by breaking up the organization through kinetic and military surface terrestrial means. It will take time to reduce the message and the attractiveness that gives it the capacity to regenerate its forces. It will take time ultimately to deny it access to the international financial system that gives it the capabilities of restoring itself or generating capabilities.

All of those things together, if we deny them that access, if we can defeat their messaging in the information sphere, and we can break them up into small groups that cannot mass to be operationally significant, then that is defeat.

Senator JOHNSON. And I am out of time. Thank you, General.

The CHAIRMAN. Thank you.

Senator Cardin.

Senator CARDIN. Thank you, Mr. Chairman. And, General Allen, thank you very much for your continued service to our country. We appreciate that very much. These are extremely challenging times, and we are very proud of your leadership.

General ALLEN. Thank you, sir.

Senator CARDIN. You are urging us to be patient, that this is going to take some time in order to achieve our mission of not only degrading, but destroying and defeating ISIL. You believe, as I understand, that the authorizations previously passed by Congress give the administration the authorization necessary for use of force. But I also understand you support the President's request to Congress?

General ALLEN. I do. I do, sir.

Senator CARDIN. And, of course, the President's request to Congress is pretty specific on ISIL and expires in 3 years. It is clear that there may well be a need for a continued military U.S. presence beyond that 3 years.

General ALLEN. I would say probably a need for military activity, U.S. activity in some form or another, yes, sir.

Senator CARDIN. And I think that is an honest assessment.

General ALLEN. Sure.

Senator CARDIN. And if I understand the reasoning behind their request is that the current administration recognizes it will be up to the next administration to come back to Congress to get the next Congress and the administration together on the continued commitment to fight terrorists and what use of force will be necessary.

General ALLEN. I cannot answer that precisely, but it would seem that is a logical reason for that.

Senator CARDIN. So my point is, why does that not also apply to 2001 authorization of force? Here we are talking about a threat that was identified last year that we are currently combating, recognizing that the campaign or use of force may well go beyond 3 years. But it is the prerogative of the next Congress and administration to define the authorizations that are needed.

The 2001 authorization, which was passed against a known threat against the United States in Afghanistan, now is still being used to a threat such as ISIL. Would the same logic not apply that Congress should define the 2001 authorization contemporary with the current needs to go after al-Qaeda?

General ALLEN. I have traveled to many of the capitals of this coalition, and one of the things that has been clear to me as I have traveled to these capitals has been the really substantial gratitude of the coalition for American leadership and the willingness for America to act. And in so many ways, these nations of the coalition see ISIL in a very different way than they ever saw al-Qaeda.

So they are grateful for our leadership. They are grateful for our willingness to act. And I believe that this AUMF, which is specifically tailored to ISIL, with the very strong support of the Congress, gives not just the President the options that are necessarily ultimately to deal with this new and unique threat, but it also reinforces the image of American leadership that is, I think, so deeply wanted by our partners, and so deeply needed by this country and ultimately by the coalition to deal with ISIL the way we want to.

Senator CARDIN. And I understand that, and it is limited to 3 years.

General ALLEN. That is right.

Senator CARDIN. Would you agree that our success in Iraq in dealing with ISIL very much depends upon the Sunni tribes taking a leadership role in stopping the advancement of ISIL, that it is difficult for the Shiites, it is difficult for Western forces to be able to get the type of confidence in the community to withstand the recruitments of ISIL?

General ALLEN. I would put it slightly differently. I would absolutely agree with you, but I think it takes decisive Sunni leadership as well within Iraq, and that leadership is coming together. But the tribes will be essential to the outcome, and your question is correct, sir.

Senator CARDIN. And what is your confidence in the Government of Iraq and Baghdad and its ability to work with the Sunni tribal leaders to give them that type confidence that their centralized government represents their interests and protects their interests?

General ALLEN. Sure. It is a hard sell, Senator, because previously we asked the Sunni tribes to trust the central government in Baghdad under Malaki. It did not work out too well for them frankly. But I have met with many of the Sheikhs of the tribes of Al-Anbar and some other of the areas of Iraq. And I have been please, frankly, very pleased at their willingness to accept the leadership of Prime Minister Abadi, and their willingness to accept the leadership of the Minister of Defense and the Minister of Interior in helping them ultimately to be one of the principal mechanisms by which we will defeat Daesh in that country.

And that has been a very encouraging sign for me, frankly, to see them not just as a group of tribes, but also as leaders of the tribes, be public and forthcoming in their willingness to support the central government in Iraq and, in particular, Prime Minister Abadi.

Senator CARDIN. Thank you, General. I really do appreciate all your service.

General ALLEN. Yes, sir. Thank you, sir.

The CHAIRMAN. Thank you, sir.

Senator Paul.

Senator PAUL. General Allen, thanks for your testimony. What percentage would you say is an estimate of how many of the officials in Iraqi are Sunni versus Shia?

General ALLEN. I will have to take the question, sir, and get back to you. Right now, the standing army, the preponderance is the majority is Shia, but I cannot give you the numbers. I will take the question——

Senator PAUL. The reason I ask is because it is sort of on the heels of what Senator Cardin is asking. Global Security reports basically somewhere between 80 to 90 percent of the official Iraqi Army being Shia. I think to have an enduring victory, there is some question from some of us whether or not you can have an enduring victory and occupy Mosul and be seen as a legitimate government if you have got an 80- to 90-percent Shia force. So I think that still is a significant political problem and a significant military problem as well.

Of the chieftains that fought in the surge, just an estimate, what percentage are engaged on our side now fighting against ISIS, and what percentage are on the sidelines, and what percentage indifferent?

General ALLEN. Again, those are numbers that are difficult to give you with any precision. The ones that I fought alongside in 2007 and 2008, the ones that I have spoken to, without exception have indicated their desire to fight Daesh to recover their lands, to ultimately return, in this case, Al-Anbar, to the tribes and ultimately to Iraq. And so, they have been very forthcoming in their desire to do that, every one that I have spoken to.

Senator PAUL. And the chieftains are no longer in the area? They have been driven out of the area, the ones that you have spo- ken——

——

General ALLEN. Well, many of them are. Some have, at great risk, traveled out of the area ultimately to speak with us. But they are, and many of them are in Amman and they are in other places.

Senator PAUL. With regard to arming the Kurds, there were reports a month or two ago that Germany wanted to send arms directly to them, but there were objections by our government saying everything had to go through Baghdad. Are arms from our allies forced to go through Baghdad to get to the Kurds?

General ALLEN. I will take the question, but let me offer this. Baghdad has not disapproved requests that the Kurds have made for weapons. We have attempted to work with Baghdad to streamline to the maximum extent possible to reduce any delays that may inhibit or impair the expeditious delivery of arms and equipment to the Kurds.

Senator PAUL. Do you think this includes sufficient technology and long-range weaponry to meet their needs and their requests?

General ALLEN. Well, all of that is coming. As you know, sir, and, again through the support of the Congress, we are training and equipping 12 Iraqi brigades, three of which are peshmerga brigades, and those peshmerga brigades will be armed and equipped with exactly the same sophisticated weapons that the other nine Iraqi brigades will receive.

Senator PAUL. We are destroying or abandoning equipment in Afghanistan. Is there any possibility that any of that could be transported to the Kurds?

General ALLEN. That is a question we should pose to the Department of Defense, but I will take the question.

Senator PAUL. Thank you. With regard to ultimate victory with regard to trying to get Turkey involved, do you think there is any possibility of an agreement between the Turks and the Kurds, particularly the Turkish Kurds, to accept an agreement where there would be a Kurdish homeland not in Turkish territory that would encourage Turkey then to participate more heavily? And is anybody in the State Department trying to come to an accommodation between the Turks and the Kurds?

General ALLEN. Not to my knowledge.

Senator PAUL. Take that message to them, too, please. Thank you.

General ALLEN. Senator, if I may, on the one comment you made with respect to the Shia and the Shia composition of the Iraqi Security Forces. The actions that will be taken in these towns are going to be more than simply those of the clearing force. What is going to be very important to recognize as well is there will be follow-on echelons behind the clearing force, which will be important as well. And we are working closely with the Iraqis for the hold force, which will be hopefully the Sunni police, which will actually secure and provide support to the Iraqi population that will have just been liberated.

The governance element, which will be familiar to those Sunni elements that will have been liberated, and, very importantly, to have the Sunnis involved in what may be the most important aspect of the clearance of Daesh out of those areas, which is the immediate humanitarian assistance necessary to provide for the relief and the recovery of the populations.

So it is more complex than simply the clearing force. And while we may have to accept that there is a large presence of the Shia elements within the Iraqi military, I know that there is a very strong effort underway to ensure that the Sunnis are deeply engaged elsewhere in all the other aspects of the recovery of the population.

Senator PAUL. And one just quick followup to that. I think you might get more indigenous support from the Sunni people if you are leafleting the place as you are invading saying it is an invading Sunni force led by Sunni generals, and that were announced. I think our problem really was Mosul was being occupied by a Shiite force, and they did not stay long. Once push came to shove, they were pretty much gone. Thanks.

The CHAIRMAN. Senator Markey.

Senator MARKEY. Thank you, Mr. Chairman, very much. Thank you, General, so much for your service.

In the authorization for the use of military force text that the administration provided to this committee, it said that it would prohibit enduring ground forces. And this was meant to convey that large numbers of troops would not be on the ground for a long time, whatever that means. I voted for the 2001 resolution, and I am reminded that the U.S. combat operations in Afghanistan were dubbed "Operation Enduring Freedom."

We are now past 13 years in that enduring fight, and that resolution, of course, was also the basis for the justification of our actions in Somalia, in Yemen. And the administration is saying quite clearly that they oppose the repeal of that, and that the operations that are going on right now, in fact, are consistent with that 2001 resolution.

Now, that causes great problems to me and, I think, to many members of the committee because even in the absence of the passage of a new AUMF, the administration is maintaining that they have the authority to continue as they have for 13 years under Operation Enduring Freedom. And so, that obviously is a problem for us because that sits there as an underlying authority for the next President, Democrat or Republican, who is sworn in on January 20, 2017. And most of us will be sitting here then as your successor is sitting here, and perhaps not with the same interpretation of the word "enduring."

So my questions then go to, is this going to open up a potential foreign open-ended war in the Middle East? Will it allow for unfettered deployment of ground troops? And ultimately, whether or not we are opening up Pandora's Box, especially in Syria. So my first question to you goes to President Assad and what the goal will be underneath this authorization in terms of the removal of President Assad, which has been historically an objective that the United States has said is important.

So could you tell us what President Assad and his removal represents as one of the goals that exists in training 5,000 troops in Syria for the next 3 years in a row as the long-term objective after the defeat of al-Nusra and ISIS?

General ALLEN. Well, our political goal, our policy goal ultimately is that the process of change, of Assad's departure should occur through a political process, and that ultimately he should depart and should not be part of the future political landscape in Syria. The role of the T&E program is to, first and foremost, to give those elements of the moderate Syrian opposition that we are supporting the capacity to defend themselves, to build battlefield credibility, and ultimately to use those elements, those forces, to deal with Daesh in the context of our strategy to deal with Daesh.

At the same time that we are building that capacity in the moderate Syrian opposition, our hope would be building within the political echelon of the moderate Syrian opposition a level of coherence and sophistication that the two together—the moderate Syrian political echelon and the military echelon—are the credible force that will have a place at the table during that political process, which will ultimately see the replacement of Assad.

Senator MARKEY. I appreciate that, but it just seems to me that that is a 10-year proposition, and if that is the case we should be talking about a 10-year period. We can finish Iraq perhaps over the next 3 years, but then in Syria it is a much longer process. And we should just understand what the long-term goal requires from us inside of Syria. And just saying Assad's name over and over again I think will just help us to focus on the ultimate objective that the Free Syrian Army is going to have in that country, and then what we are signing up for in terms of the long-term military effort inside of that country.

And I thank you, Mr. Chairman, for the opportunity to ask this one final question, which is, the basic tension that King Abdullah was talking about, which is that of the Americans providing help to fight the war, but not claiming credit so it does not look like a crusade inside of that region. Can you talk about that so that the people in the region do not view this as a U.S.-led coalition against ISIL, because ultimately that then comes back to haunt us. And that was the message that we are receiving from all the Middle East.

General ALLEN. Well, I think, Senator, as your question pre-supposes, King Abdullah of Jordan has been very clear throughout the period of this coalition that in the end the solution to the problems of the region must not only look like, but must be a function of those states within the region to take concerted action supported by the United States and supported by a broader global coalition for those concerted actions to be successful.

It is very important obviously that the solution have an Arab face and a Muslim voice with respect to dealing with the so-called caliphate and all that it has brought to the region. And the king and other Muslim and Arab leaders in the region have been very clear on the desire that they not just appear, but really are exercising leadership frontally in this process.

Senator MARKEY. I do not think people in that region view it that way right now. I think that has to be our goal, though. We just have to switch it so that it is not us, and I think Senator Paul is referring to that, that it has to be an indigenous Muslim-led effort, and I do not think that is the internal view.

Thank you.

The CHAIRMAN. Thank you.

Senator Isakson.

Senator ISAKSON. Thank you, Mr. Chairman. General Allen, thank you for your service to the country. I have followed you on TV closely the last couple of months, and I think you have done a great job.

General ALLEN. Thank you, sir.

Senator ISAKSON. Am I correct, we are operating currently in the Middle East under the 2001 AUMF? Is that correct?

General ALLEN. Yes, sir. That is correct.

Senator ISAKSON. Would it be a fair statement to say the one the President has sent to us to consider is actually a limiting AUMF compared to the 2001 authorization?

General ALLEN. It is specifically intended to deal with the threat of ISIL. That is correct.

Senator ISAKSON. But it is limiting in the authority the President would have primarily by the interpretation of the ''enduring'' phrase. Is that correct?

General ALLEN. ''Enduring'' and the expectation, as he has described it in the proposed legislation, on the size and the kinds of forces that might be applied, measures that be applied. That is correct.

Senator ISAKSON. Like Senator Markey, I voted for the 2001 authorization when I was here. It came on the heels of 9/11/2001. It was passed at a time when Americans had American flags on their windshields and their front doors, and American businesses had flags raised. And the patriotism in our country, because of the terrible attack against our country, was at an all-time high, at least in my lifetime, in my memory. Are we going to have to wait for that type of event again to happen to us before we use whatever it takes to destroy this evil, meaning ISIL and those like them?

General ALLEN. I think we are taking those measures now to get after the evil that is ISIL, and it is an evil we have not seen before in a very long time. Just today the FBI rolled up three individuals in this country that were intent of either joining or doing—joining ISIL in the battle space or doing ill to the American people. And as long as we are the front edge of this and taking those kinds of measures, I think we have the possibility of keeping it from becoming something that could like a 9/11.

Senator ISAKSON. In your printed statement, and I assume it is part of your remarks that you said verbally, you said, ''It will ultimately be the aggregate pressure of the coalition's activity over multiple mutual supporting lines of effort that will determine the campaign's success.''

General ALLEN. That is correct, sir.

Senator ISAKSON. What are those mutually supporting lines that you are referring to?

General ALLEN. First, working very closely within the coalition and more broadly in the community of nations to limit the flow of foreign fighters; to deal with the measures—to take the measures necessary to deal with the ability to limit ISIL's capacity to generate revenue, ultimately to support its operations, and to give it discretion to take action against us or potentially our allies; to provide support to those elements of the population in the region that have been displaced by virtue of the activities of ISIL or have been directly suppressed by the boot of ISIL's conquests and subjugation; and then, very importantly, to work together in the information space ultimately to defeat the idea of Daesh.

And the coalition is working very hard in those areas. I have just come back from Southeast Asia where I met with the leadership of several countries there. They are watching with great interest and concern those things that are—that are occurring in the Middle East which could spread into their region. And they are interested in joining us in ways that can limit the ability of those organizations there to travel to the battle space or to limit their ability to directly challenge the authorities of those countries. So it is not just the countries of the Middle East. It is not just the countries of Europe. It is the countries of Southeast Asia.

And very importantly within the context of the multiple lines of effort, working very closely to outreach to the indigenous populations of these countries in ways that can dispel the image of this so-called caliphate in ways that we can work with religious leaders and tribal leaders in those countries with populations that may be at risk. Work with teachers, and clerics, and families to reduce the attractiveness of Daesh and this kind of an extremist message.

And the combination of all those activities together we think will pressure and ultimately put the kinds of pressure necessary on Daesh, first, to defend ourselves, and ultimately to defeat the organization.

Senator ISAKSON. On that point and very briefly because my time will be up in about 45 seconds.

General ALLEN. Yes, sir.

Senator ISAKSON. Are we doing enough to counteract the use of social media and technology to communicate exactly what you are talking about that they are doing, because what you heard about in Southeast Asia and what I have heard from on some trips I have taken is the fear they will use social media and the modern communication mechanisms that we have today to spread their ideology and their fear around the world. Are we attacking that as much as we should?

General ALLEN. They are doing it now, and it is, in fact, an explicit objective within our efforts within the counter messaging line of effort among the many nations involved to do just that. Obviously in nations where free speech is an issue, we have to accommodate that aspect of our relationship with industry that own these platforms to ensure that we are either able to interdict that message or with industry to remove that message within its own content. So we are working very closely actually with industry and with our partners to counter that message across all the social media.

Senator ISAKSON. Thank you for your time and your service.

General ALLEN. Thank you, sir.

The CHAIRMAN. Thank you.

Senator Boxer.

Senator BOXER. Thank you so much, Mr. Chairman, Ranking Member Menendez. General, thank you so much for your dedication to this nation. I want to thank the President for the wisdom he showed in appointing you as the special envoy. I find your presentation to be very direct, no frills, just straightforward, and I appreciate it.

Under Article 1, Section 8, Congress has the power to declare war. I know you agree with that, yes?

General ALLEN. Yes, ma'am.

Senator BOXER. All right. So I hope you could then understand why we want to be very precise when we do that because we are sent here by a lot of people who have a lot of kids who serve in the military, and they are the fabric of our community, so we want to be careful. And I just want to say—I am not even going to ask you to expand on this ''enduring'' word because you have said it very clearly. Your definition of no enduring presence could mean a 2-week presence of combat boots on the ground, American boots on the ground, or a 2-year presence of American combat boots on the ground.

And that answers the question the Democrats on this committee have been searching for—this definition—and I think what you have proven with your honesty here is there is no definition because it is in the eye of the beholder. When you say to me that if I vote for this there will be no enduring combat presence, and I am sending kids in my State there for 2 years, I would argue you have misinterpreted it. The Congressional Research Service says there is really no definition. And if I wanted to take an administration to court because as a Member of Congress, I said no enduring presence, CRS says I would not have a legal leg to stand on because there is no definition.

So I just think it is very important the administration hear this once again. I mean, I know poor Secretary Kerry had to hear it over and over again from our side yesterday, but we are very uncomfortable with this language. And when Senator Menendez was chairman, he cobbled together a really good AUMF that united all of us on our side because he essentially said no combat troops with these exceptions, and he put in the kind of exceptions I think you would agree with: special forces operations, search and rescue, protecting personnel. And we would urge you to please go back and take a look at it. I just feel very strongly.

Now, I want to ask you questions that have nothing to do with that because I think you and I would probably disagree on that subject. There is no point in going over it again. But I am very concerned about U.S. military support for the Kurds, and you answered the question in a very sure way, which is wonderful. You said, oh, no problem. However, the Kurds are not saying that.

So I want to call to your attention a recent interview with Bloomberg View just 3 weeks ago. The head of the Kurdistan Regional Security Council expressed concerns about our commitment to the Kurds, and these are our boots on the ground. These are our boots on the ground. He said, ''We are starting to have doubts that there might be a political decision on what sort of equipment should be given to the Kurds . . . We are fighting on behalf of the rest of the world against this terrorist organization. We are putting our lives on the line. All we ask for is the sufficient equipment to protect these lives.''

So I need you to respond to that. Is that off base? What do you think about that? Do you take that comment seriously? Does it concern you?

General ALLEN. Well, I listen very carefully to what the Kurds have to say, and they have, in so many ways, demonstrated battlefield excellence and courage that should elicit all of our respect. But we have worked very carefully and very closely with the Kurds, and your question presupposes, and is correct, that American support to the Kurds has given them the capacity, and more broadly and more recently, coalition support to the Kurds has given them the ability to do much of what they have been able to accomplish: the recovery of Mosul Dam, the seizure of Kisik Junction, the successful defense of Guerra. The many things that they have done is because the coalition has been in close support with them.

At the same time, in several different rounds we have worked very hard with coalition members to respond to Kurdish requests for equipment, and that equipment has been flowing in. Also, in the context of the $1.6 billion that was appropriated for the train and equip program for the 12 Iraqi army brigades, three of which are peshmerga, they are getting exactly the same sophisticated equipment that the Kurds or the Iraqis are getting.

Senator BOXER. My question was not about how good they are. We agree. They are saying they do not feel they have enough equipment. And I am just saying that while you are saying everything is rosy, they are complaining about it. And I just want to say—as one Senator, I cannot speak for anyone else—they are our boots on the ground, and we need to get them what they need. I know there is pressure from certain factions, but if they are going to be our boots on the ground, we have got to give them what they need. Thank you.

The CHAIRMAN. Thank you.

Senator Rubio.

Senator RUBIO. Thank you. First of all, General, thank you for your service to our country and for your willingness to come back in and help with this new endeavor of great difficulty.

I want to start out by just—I know we are not debating the authorization for use of force, but I do want to ask you because of your experience in these affairs in the past, it is my understanding from our review of the process that only two times in our history has Congress authorized the use of force with limitations, and both were United Nations peacekeeping missions. And so, the question that I would have now is, if our objective here is the defeat of ISIS, would it not be more prudent to authorize the Commander in Chief to move forward in that regard and allow him as Commander in Chief and any future Commander in Chief, whoever they may be, to decide what the appropriate strategy is moving forward to ultimately defeat them if that is the ultimate goal? What would be wrong with simply authorizing the President to defeat them?

General ALLEN. Well, the strategy that the President has approved, in fact, does envision the defeat of Daesh.

Senator RUBIO. No, I understand the strategy does. Just for purposes of an authorization from Congress, and I understand you have endorsed here today what the President wants to do, and I understand that perhaps that is what the President thinks he can get passed. But from a military point of view, would it not be more appropriate to simply authorize the President to do whatever it takes to defeat them?

General ALLEN. The President needs the options that he—that should be available to him ultimately to defeat Daesh.

Senator RUBIO. Okay. My second question is, is it possible to defeat ISIS without them ultimately being defeated by someone on the ground? Someone is going to have to confront them eventually on the ground and defeat them there. If you can update us on efforts, and I have seen in the past some conversation among some of the regional countries, about the potential for a coalition of armed forces brought together—the Egyptians, the Turks, the Saudis, perhaps some of the kingdoms, Jordan, et cetera—who could provide a coalition of local forces who could play that role with significant U.S. assistance from the air, logistics, intelligence, et cetera. Has there been any progress made in that? Is that something that is actively being discussed with those nations?

General ALLEN. Senator Rubio, I would really prefer to have this particular part of the conversation in a closed session.

Senator RUBIO. Okay, I understand. So let me move on then to a separate topic, and that is the nature of this conflict. ISIS has already proven that they are going to move into—for a group to take root, and take hold, and actually be able to grow, they need ungoverned vacuum spaces that they can operate from. That is what perhaps has attracted them, for example, to Libya, not just the access to a port town, but the ability to operate uncontested in terms of another government, et cetera.

It is important to understand that as this conflict continues, the possibility continues to grow that ISIS, in addition to being based in Syria and Iraq, will also look to other places where they can set up nodes operation. Libya is an example, but potentially training camps in Afghanistan. Any place where a vacuum opens up is an attractive and appealing place for them to move operations.

And, therefore, as we put forth our strategy and as the Congress deliberates the authority it gives the President, that reality needs to be taken into account, correct?

General ALLEN. I agree, yes, sir.

Senator RUBIO. Okay. My last question is about the nature of this conflict. You know, it has been talked about in the past that ISIS is some sort of, and they certainly are, a group of monsters that take on these acts of extreme violence, but these are not just random acts of extreme violence. This is a group who has a—their barbarism has a purpose. At the end of the day it is to purify, in their mind, that region to their form of Islam at the exclusion not just of non-Sunni Islam, but especially of non-Islamic populations.

And in that realm, it is clear that the Christians and Yazidis, but recently we have seen Christians in particular, are in increased danger in this region, and they specifically target Christian populations for barbarity, both as a way to shock the world, but also as an effort to carry out their ultimate goal of, in their mind, ''purifying the region for Islam.'' Is there a not deep religious component to ISIS' strategy here? They are clearly as part of their effort trying to, again, using a term they would use, not one that I necessarily enjoy using, but ''cleanse the region'' of infidels and non-believers. And in that realm they have specifically targeted Christians for these sorts of atrocities that they are committing on now an ongoing basis as we saw yesterday again.

General ALLEN. I would say yes to that. The interpretation that they apply to all of those segments of the population that live within the area that they control has permitted them to do the things that they have done to certain elements of the population. So I absolutely agree with you. Their interpretation of their responsibility under this so-called caliphate is to take action against certain elements of the population and treat them one way, and certain elements of the population and treat them another way. It is based on their historic interpretation.

The CHAIRMAN. Thank you.

Senator Kaine.

Senator KAINE. Thank you, Mr. Chairman, and thank you, General Allen, for your service. I also want to thank you. You did very significant and important work with respect to trying to provide a security roadmap for the West Bank in the event of a peace deal between Israeli and Palestinian leaders. Whether the leaders will do what their citizens want them to do and find such a deal is up to them. But it should not go unnoticed that you worked very, very hard on that, and you have put in place a template for security on the West Bank that is a very good thing in your work then, and in this context, really in the best traditions of American diplomacy. And I want to thank you for that.

General ALLEN. Thank you, sir.

Senator KAINE. I want to make a comment about ends in the next two questions about means. I will pick up—Senator Johnson was quizzing you about what is defeat of ISIL. They are not a state. They say they are a state. They are not. They are not Islamic. They say they are. They are not. They are a mutation of Islam. And you even talk about defeating the idea of ISIL. I agree with you. They are just sort of an ideologically driven death cult.

And so, as we grapple with the authorization, we really have to kind of grapple with this question of what does defeat look like. I am very practical about this. I want to protect Americans from ISIL. That is what I want to do. I want to protect Americans from ISIL, and I want to protect our allies who ask for our help. The defeat of the ideology, the death cult, you know, fantasy that they had, we could be chasing after a phantom by trying to do that. But I want to protect Americans, and I want to defend our allies who ask us for that.

On the means side, a question about the ground troops issues. In the last three weeks, we have had meetings with two leaders from the region, King Abdullah and today the emir of Qatar. King Abdullah said this is our fight, not yours, and basically suggested that U.S. ground troops would not be a good idea. The emir of Qatar was actually even more straightforward about that today. He said I do not want American ground troops in. He actually—we did not suggest this to him. He brought up the notion that American ground troops may be a recruiting bonanza for ISIL, may change the notion of what the fight is. It is against the West, now we can really recruit people.

General ALLEN. I think that is accurate.

Senator KAINE. And so, this is—you know, the ground troop thing is a wordsmithing issue, but the wordsmithing is subsidiary to the bigger issue, which is, you know, do we become an occupier? Do we become a recruiting tool for ISIL? King Abdullah's notion, you know. This terrorism is born and bred in the region. The United States did not create it. The region has got to stand up against it. If the region is not willing to stand up against it, there is virtually nothing that the United States can do, no matter how many resources we put into it, that will ultimately lead to a success. We cannot police the region that will not police itself.

So I am kind of interested—forget about the wordsmithing. But when the leaders from the region say American ground troops are a bad idea, that is pretty—that is a powerful thought to those of us who are going to be voting on the authorization. How would you respond to that notion that the presence of any significant American ground troops changes the character of this and makes it the West against ISIL rather than a region needing to police its own extremism?

General ALLEN. Well, I do agree with both the emir and the king. The presence, the infusion of a large—and I think this where they would be a little more precise if given the opportunity. The presence of a large conventional maneuver force would change the nature of the conversation. But it is really important to understand that during Iraq, and during Afghanistan, and in the way we have responded to other similar challenges around the world, the United States brings to bear a variety of really important capabilities.

The first is the capacity of our strategic leadership. Just our leadership alone has brought to bear 62 nations against this challenge. Our leadership brought to bear the first night of our strike operations five Arab air forces flying along on the wing of the United States Air Force in strikes against ISIL targets in Syria. That is not anything that any of us could have imagined a year ago. So our strategic leadership counts as really an enabler to this process.

Other ways and means, and your question is really important. Other ways and means that we can bring success to the Arab solution to this is providing technical support, intelligence support; focused special operations strike capabilities; the training and equipping that we are doing today, some of which can be done in country, some of which can be done offshore in partner nations; the aggregation of those activities undertaken with partners in the region ultimately to achieve the ends that we seek.

The United States really has and our coalition partners really have many means at our disposal from leadership all the way through to potential for special operations strike to give our Arab partners exactly what they want, which is the capacity for them to be the defeat mechanism in the end of Daesh.

Senator KAINE. Thank you, Mr. Chairman.

Senator FLAKE [presiding]. Senator Gardner.

Senator GARDNER. Thank you, Mr. Chairman, and thank you, General Allen, for your service, and your time, and your testimony today. And, again, we have to recognize that ISIS is a real threat to this country, and it requires a comprehensive strategy. And the commitment to their total destruction, I think, is the only thing that we can accept.

I am glad the President has made the effort to forward the AUMF to Congress. Obviously I look forward to working with the President on the AUMF and this committee. In the letter that the President transmitted along with his language in the AUMF, he stated ''I have directed a comprehensive and sustained strategy to degrade and defeat ISIL. As part of this strategy, U.S. military forces are conducting a systematic campaign of airstrikes against ISIL in Iraq and Syria.''

It is my understanding from the testimony that you have provided to us today that the United States has conducted about 2,500 airstrikes. Is that correct?

General ALLEN. That is correct, sir.

Senator GARDNER. And that is since Operation Inherent Resolve began on August 8. That is the timeframe of the 2,500?

General ALLEN. Yes, sir.

Senator GARDNER. Okay. And that is an average of 10 airstrikes a day. And so, the question I have is, is the pace of the operation sufficient to eradicate ISIL at this point?

General ALLEN. Well, eradication is not the end state that we are seeking at this particular moment. Our hope—''hope'' is not the term I want to use. What our expectation is given the strategy is that the combination of U.S. and coalition air power in conjunction with the training and equipping of Iraqi Forces and ultimately Syrian forces will over time give us the strategic outcomes that we desire. That is not going to happen tomorrow. It is going to happen over a period of time. But the combination of all those things together is what we anticipate will permit us to achieve the objectives of the strategy.

Senator GARDNER. And so, what besides the airstrikes then does the President's comprehensive and sustained strategy envision?

General ALLEN. Several things. The first is to provide support to the stability of the Iraqi Government, which is essential, and we are doing that. We are working closely with the Iraqi Government with respect to reforms in partnership with the Abadi government, which is inclined to see it that way. Working closely with the Iraqi Security Forces to prepare ultimately for a long-term counter offensive, which will remove Daesh from the population centers and ultimately eject it from the country.

We are working as an international coalition on behalf of Iraq to pressure Daesh's capacities to generate funds and resources necessary for its long-term survival. We are working as an international coalition to staunch the flow of foreign fighters to the battlefield so that Daesh has difficulty in replacing its combat losses. We are going to work very closely as partners to share intelligence so that we are working with the Iraqis to give them a clear picture of what we understand Daesh to be, but also between and among the members of the coalition that we can defend ourselves and our homelands from the potential for Daesh activities within the United States.

And then, of course, we are working very closely with our partners to provide humanitarian assistance to those elements of the population that will need to be recovered and relieved as we liberate them from the presence of Daesh in their population centers. And then finally, to work together with Iraq and our partners to deal what I think is the decisive blow here beyond the physical defeat of Daesh, which is the defeat of its idea and the idea of its attractiveness over the long term.

Senator GARDNER. And the pace of operations which we discussed, with the passage of the AUMF, does that change at all?

General ALLEN. Well, I think the pace of the operation will be judged as time goes. You know, commanders take stock of the operational environment, and ultimately resource the operations that either—takes advantage of opportunities that are availed to them by the changes in the operational environment. We could well find that based on our current estimates that the activities that we will undertake in the counter offensive will follow along the pace and the timeline that we anticipate. But we could easily find that as the counter offensive unfolds, that Daesh is unwilling to receive defeat after defeat at the hands of the Iraqi Security Forces, which is exactly what we want to see. And they may decide that it is time to pull out.

So we may see that the operational environment could change, and it is the responsibility of our very capable commanders, in this case, Lloyd Austin and James Terry, to constantly be monitoring the success of the unfolding operation to ensure we are getting the most out of the resources that we have, and if we need more resources, that we ask for them.

Senator GARDNER. Thank you, Mr. Chairman.

Senator FLAKE. Senator Murphy.

Senator MURPHY. Thank you very much, Mr. Chairman. General Allen, thank you for your service. Thank you for your answers to the questions. I agree with Senator Boxer, they are straightforward and very helpful.

I want to build on some questions from Senator Menendez and Senator Boxer on the authorizing language that we have before us. A lot of attention has been given to this phrase ''enduring,'' not as much attention given to the juxtaposition that has now been created between what are offensive forces and what are defensive forces. Just so I understand this, you have talked about what the potential limitation is on size of force or duration of force under the enduring limitation. But so long as the presence of troops is considered defensive, there is no limitation in this authorization of military as to the number of troops or the duration of their time in the conflict area so long as they are considered defensive forces.

General ALLEN. Again, I am not sponsoring the legislation, but I think your point is correct in that regard. It is about offensive maneuver forces.

Senator MURPHY. I thought your answer to Senator Kaine's question was definitive in that you worry, as I know the President does, that a large-scale deployment of troops could become recruiting fodder for extremists as our presence in Iraq did over the 10 years. Do you think that that changes if our categorization of the forces are offensive or defensive, if we have 100,000 defensive troops? I do not think this President is going to authorize this, but this is a 3-year authorization, so the next President will get the chance to decide differently.

Would it matter in terms of the ability for extremists to recruit as to whether our troops there were categorized as defensive versus offensive?

General ALLEN. Again, these are all individual measures. It depends on how the crisis has unfolded. It depends on the region in which those forces may be involved. It would depend on the activities that may have occurred prior to the introduction of forces that we might call defensive. It is just not possible to give a specific answer to that question. You know, I would have a difficult time understanding how we would have 100,000 forces in a defensive environment if we had not had substantial offensive operations to begin with. And that would, of course, change the regional view and the perspective on our forces and the outcome.

So I think that there will be occasions where we may find that locations or facilities or concentrations of friends and allies need to be defended. The rationale that we would use with our regional partners for the insertion of our allied troops to defend those locations or those populations would be very, very important. And so, I think each region or each of those circumstances would have to be judged independently.

Senator MURPHY. And do you have a sense, and I know you are not the sponsor of this legislation, but you were there, as to what the limits of that word ''defensive'' are? If our forces were there taking fire from an ISIL position and needed to advance on that position to eliminate it in order to defend our troops, I assume that that action in that time and space looking like an offensive action would still be considered defensive in the sense that it was necessary in order to defend our troops or coalition troops?

General ALLEN. Well, yes. In that particular example, yes. Again, we would probably prior to the deployment of those forces have come forward with as clear an explanation as we could as to what defensive would look in the context of accomplishing that mission and accomplishing those tasks associated with defense.

Senator MURPHY. You are going to get stuck with a lot of hypothetical questions on these two phrases ''enduring'' and ''defensive and offensive'' simply because we are stuck with them trying to figure them out.

Just one last question if I could. Part of the success of the awakening was not just persuasion, but also the transfer of substantial resources to tribes. We, you know, effectively paid tribes in various ways in order to compensate them for their moving away from insurgencies and towards coalition forces. What did we learn from that experience, and how does it educate us as we try to move forward a strategy, once again, of trying to win over these forces?

General ALLEN. That is a really important question. I was eye deep in that process.

Senator MURPHY. Yes.

General ALLEN. And we did, in fact, provide direct support. And we gave that direct support to the tribes in so many ways because a central government was incapable of doing it. And when we provided that support and ultimately the tribes made the strategic decision to side with us against al-Qaeda, as you well recall, fundamentally the operation al environment changed very quickly in 2007 and 2008.

I think what we learned from that was not the fundamental change in the battle space that favored us. It was the long-term outcome of the Sons of Iraq, which was the handover of the responsibility to resource the Sons of Iraq to the central government in Iraq. And that did not work out frankly because it was never clear to us, I think, whether Malaki intended to support them or not.

So in this case, and the lesson is being applied today. In this case, we seek in every possible way both to encourage and to support the central government to build those bridges now with the tribal elements by providing support to them, by being present in the training process, and ultimately ensuring the linkage between the Sheikhs and the Iraqi civilian Sunni leaders, that linkage now is effective with the central government, not in a handoff later. And that one of the important messages or lessons that have come out of this.

Senator MURPHY. And so, does that include financial resources being transferred from the Iraqi Government to these tribes? Is that one of our recommendations to them?

General ALLEN. Yes, in the context, for example, of the 2015 budget that was just passed by the Iraqis. There was a wedge in there for the recruitment of tribal elements and indigenous populations from each province into the national guard organizations. And those national guard organizations will belong to the governor.

They will support the police locally in the event that there is a crisis, or will be nationalized, federalized to support the army in the event of a national emergency.

That entity will belong to the ministry of defense. They will recruited into the Ministry of Defense. They will be part of the national guard brigade, but they will be paid by national funds. So the mechanisms underway right now where we are training tribal elements in Al-Anbar, for example, they are actually being paid now by the Iraqi Government and armed by the Iraqi Government. We are providing the training.

Senator MURPHY. Thank you.

General ALLEN. Yes, sir.

The CHAIRMAN [presiding]. Thank you.

Senator Flake.

Senator FLAKE. Thank you. Thank you for your testimony. We have got a vote on, so I need to go quickly, so I will ask just a couple of questions quickly.

How important do you think, and I apologize if you answered this before I came. How important do you think it is to have the AUMF?

General ALLEN. It is very important.

Senator FLAKE. How important—go ahead.

General ALLEN. I think it is extraordinarily important actually. The United States has exerted great leadership in bringing together these countries ultimately to support the restoration of the situation in Iraq, its territorial integrity and sovereignty, and ultimately to help to deal with the—to be able to defeat that Daesh necessary in Syria. So it is very important.

ISIL is a threat that is unique in our time. It is certainly unique in the time that I have been in the service. And while the elements of the AUMF will be properly debated between this body and the administration, and many of the members here today have brought up important points for clarity or for continued discussion, I think that it is extraordinarily important, the message that it sends that the administration is in a conversation and dialogue with this committee and the Congress on the issue.

But most importantly, in support of the U.S. leadership globally on this issue, a strong bipartisan vote to support the AUMF complements the leadership that the United States has exerted in this crisis.

Senator FLAKE. Well, thank you. That is certainly the case I have made that both our adversaries and our allies need to know that we speak with one voice here.

General ALLEN. That is exactly right.

Senator FLAKE. Is there one that is more important than the other in that regard, or is it equally important for both of them to hear this message?

General ALLEN. Our friends who are in the coalition in the 21 capitals I have traveled to have been extraordinarily grateful for the American leadership on this issue. What I want is for our adversaries to not be able to sleep at night because we have the unqualified support of the Congress in our actions necessary to defeat this enemy.

Senator FLAKE. At what point is the impact of this AUMF diminished if we have language that is just—I mean, if we try to include every point of view and every nuance as opposed to something straightforward that we are in this to win. At what point does it become less important?

General ALLEN. It would be difficult for me to answer, Senator, but I would just hope that the consultation between the administration and this committee puts the language in there that the President needs to defend the American people, defend our country, but also to deal the defeat to Daesh that it desperately needs.

Senator FLAKE. In other examples of AUMF, there has not been much change. We have basically done what the administration has asked for. And there have been some amendments in recent AUMFs, but by and large it has been rather straightforward language, rather short. I frankly think the language the administration put forward is a good start, and maybe amended some. But I would caution the committee and the Congress in general, the Senate and the House, from going too far to make it all things to everyone, and probably diminish the importance of it.

But anyway, thank you for your service, and thank you for your testimony here.

General ALLEN. Thank you, sir.

The CHAIRMAN. Thank you, Senator. Senator Kaine I know had a followup.

Senator KAINE. General, I wanted to ask about one of the lines of effort that we are working on in a fairly significant way, and that is the humanitarian relief line. The United States is the most generous nation in the world in terms of humanitarian relief to refugees from Syria. But the problem is getting worse in some ways because of the closing of borders with Lebanon. There were too many refugees there. Jordan, probably the same thing. Turkey with border issues is probably less willing to just see waves and waves of Syrians coming over. And so, what are we doing in tandem with the London Eleven and other nations to try to deal with the humanitarian crisis of all of these displaced folks in Syria, whether they are being displaced because of Bashar al-Assad, ISIL, cholera outbreaks, weather, desperate poverty that they are being displaced? And I wonder about or humanitarian efforts in tandem with other nations.

General ALLEN. I will give you a partial answer, sir, and I will take the question and give you the ability of the Department to come back. We obviously take that very seriously. We have the relief efforts that, as you properly point out, have been very generously supported by the United States and others directly to the populations of Syria and Iraq. We have the U.N. appeals, which need a lot more assistance to bring those appeals up to 100 percent. We are in the depth of a winter right now which has made this more urgent and more timely.

We have the frontline states that are struggling with the influx of Syrian refugees—Turkey, Lebanon, and Jordan—so we need to work closely with them to give them the kinds of support necessary to ensure that these demographic changes that they are experiencing in their countries are not in the end destabilizing to their stability and their security.

And then, very importantly, is humanitarian assistance that will follow in trace of the counter offensive when that ultimately kicks off. It can be argued that the clearing operation will be important to remove Daesh out of the population centers and the police will secure the population. But we are going to find that these people have lived under indescribable conditions, and so our ability to marshal and quickly apply the humanitarian assistance necessary to the female populations, to, more broadly, the liberated populations, to the internally displaced persons that will come home as we begin to clear these population centers of Daesh, supporting their return to their homes, the necessary humanitarian assistance to the restoration of the central services, electricity, water, and then ultimately reconstruction.

As your question presupposes, this is a huge bill, and it is a huge regional undertaking. And so, I think it should be to everyone's satisfaction, or at least optimism, many of the members of the coalition have been very clear in their willingness to support the broader U.N. effort for the region and the frontline states. And a number of the other coalition members have put their hands in the air to be leaders of and supporters to that very important humanitarian effort that will follow right closely on the heels of the clearing operation that will move Daesh out of Iraq.

So it is a multifaceted, multilayer, complex issue, but in the end the humanitarian piece, I think, is one of the death blows that Daesh will experience.

Senator KAINE. I know in response to a question from the chairman, you indicated the complexities of no-fly zones. I just would commend the idea of a humanitarian zone inside Syria probably on the border with Turkey or the border with Jordan, or maybe both, that would be justified by a U.N. Security Council resolutions already in place promoting cross-border delivery of humanitarian aid. That would be humanitarian zones for people who, whether they are fleeing Bashar al-Assad, ISIL, cholera, hunger, winter, whatever is, once the borders have been closed and they cannot transit across the borders, I hope we would contemplate some form of safe haven for the citizens who are suffering so badly in what I think most have testified is the worst refugee crisis since World War II.

General ALLEN. That is correct, sir.

Senator KAINE. Thank you, Mr. Chairman.

The CHAIRMAN. And that would be in the form of some type of no-fly zone——

Senator KAINE. Because no-fly has the military, you know, label right up front, I would call it a humanitarian safe haven zone. But definitely I would want such a zone to be protected from whoever might try to mess around with people who are refugees who are just seeking safety, yes.

The CHAIRMAN. Very good. Well, General, I know you have got a hard stop in 20 minutes, and I think we have—you have certainly helped us in the way that we wanted you to help us. We appreciate your testimony.

I would have one question, and that is you, in response to Senator Flake, talked about the need for Congress to be behind the effort that is taking place with ISIL. There have been differing discussions about the length of time from an AUMF standpoint. And is there anything about the timeframe—I know the President has asked for three—whether it is longer, shorter? Is there anything about that that you think matters at all relative to those that you are talking about appealing to our enemies and allies together?

General ALLEN. Well, our intent with respect to Daesh is to end its abilities, to deal that defeat to them as quickly as we can. If it takes longer than three years, my suspicion would be that we would come back to this committee and request an extension.

The CHAIRMAN. And if it was shorter than that, it would trouble you either.

General ALLEN. If it was shorter than that, it would not trouble me at all if Daesh were defeated in less than 3 years.

The CHAIRMAN. No, no, no, it would not trouble us either. Thank you. Does the length of time really particularly matter to you from the standpoint of the allies and those that we are defeating, or is it just more Congress getting behind the effort in a bipartisan way?

General ALLEN. Well, I think it is the latter.

The CHAIRMAN. Yes. Well, listen, I called you over the weekend when I knew you were on your way to Kuwait. I know you are your way to CENTCOM now. I think you can tell by the respect that everyone has shown you today we all view you as someone who is an outstanding public servant. We appreciate the way you have gone about your work.

I know it is difficult. I know that decisions do not always get made in the manner or in the timeframe that someone like you that wants to seek this—get this done in the appropriate way. But I think your demeanor, the way you talk with all of us is certainly very, very well received. We wish you well in what you are doing, and hope you will be before us again soon to update us.

General ALLEN. Honored to be with you today, Chairman.

The CHAIRMAN. Thank you.

General ALLEN. Thank you, sir.

The CHAIRMAN. Thank you.

General ALLEN. Have a good day, sir.

The CHAIRMAN. And with that, the record will be open until Friday for any questions.

The CHAIRMAN. We would ask that you and your staff respond to those in a fairly timely fashion.

And the meeting is adjourned.

[Whereupon, at 3:13 p.m., the hearing was adjourned.]

RESPONSES OF GEN. JOHN R. ALLEN TO QUESTIONS
SUBMITTED BY SENATOR BOB CORKER

Question. Can you please explain the command structure for the fight against ISIS? Do you believe there is a coherent chain of command aligning all elements of American and coalition power against the threat?

Answer. Because the answer to this question is outside the Department of State's purview, we must respectfully defer to the Department of Defense for a response.

Question. Do you believe an authorization for the use of force should include authority to strike the Syrian regime?

Answer. The President has been clear that he wants to work with Congress on a bipartisan, ISIL-specific AUMF. That is the immediate focus. Consistent with that focus, the administration's proposed AUMF would provide authority for the military mission we are currently undertaking in Iraq and Syria against ISIL.

We believe that Assad has lost the legitimacy to govern, but we are not asking for authority to use force against the Assad regime.

The nature and extent of the support the United States is prepared to provide to the Syrian forces we train is critically important and under active consideration. We plan to provide a level of support that is sufficient to support the objectives of the T&E program.

Question. Do you believe an authorization for the use of force should be limited by time?

Answer. The President's goal is to secure the passage of a bipartisan, limited, ISIL-specific AUMF that will provide a clear signal to the American people, to our allies, and to our enemies that the United States stands united behind the effort to degrade and ultimately defeat ISIL. The President has developed and transmitted to the Congress an AUMF that reflects bipartisan input and contains reasonable limitations and that provides the flexibility he needs to successfully pursue the armed conflict against ISIL.

Although the confrontation with ISIL will not be over quickly, the President believes that 3 years is an appropriate period of time in order to allow the next President, the Congress, and the American people to assess the progress we have made against ISIL and review the authorities we have in place.

Question. Do you believe Shia militias in Iraq are, or will be, a threat to Americans in Iraq?

Answer. The protection of our people is paramount. That is why the Department of State and the Department of Defense have taken precautions to mitigate a wide range of risks in Iraq to the level where our personnel can operate safely and effectively. Our Embassy and consulates in Iraq maintain a strong and robust security posture in Iraq and we work closely with the Department of Defense on contingency planning. Security at the missions in Iraq include Diplomatic Security Special Agents, Security Protective Specialists, Marine Security Guards, Marine Security Augmentation Unit personnel, Worldwide Protective Service armed movement security and static personnel, local guards, and host nation security forces. We refer you to Department of Defense for details about their specific security previsions at coalition military sites in Iraq.

Shia volunteers are an important element of the fighting force against ISIL inside Iraq. Although some of these groups predate the current crisis, many of these militia forces formed last summer as a result of Grand Ayatollah Sistani's call for volunteers when Baghdad and other major cities were under imminent threat. They have since continued to play a key role in the Government of Iraq's efforts to retake its sovereign territory from ISIL.

However, given the history of some of these groups targeting U.S. personnel and facilities in Iraq prior to 2012, as well as recent allegations of abuses against Iraqi civilians, we do have concerns about some of these militias. We have a continuing dialogue with the Iraqi Government about these concerns and the necessity for all militias to be brought under the command and control of the Iraqi security forces.

Prime Minister Abadi has stated that he has a zero tolerance policy of human rights abuses and all armed groups and militias should be incorporated under state security structures. The draft National Guard law approved by the Council of Ministers on February 3 is a step toward this objective, and, once implemented, an Iraqi National Guard structure will ensure greater oversight and regulation of these armed elements.

Question. How does the administration define success in Iraq and Syria? Can you explain the terms defeat, destroy, disable and contain as they relate to an end state in Iraq and Syria? Which terms align best with the administration's goals in Iraq and Syria?

Answer. Our Counter-ISIL strategy aims to degrade ISIL in Iraq and Syria over the course of a multiyear timeframe, leading to its eventual defeat.

Degrading ISIL involves suppressing its ability to conduct large-scale operations. In the immediate to medium term, conducting military operations to halt and reverse ISIL's territorial expansion; reducing its capability to resource, plan and execute offensive and/or terrorist attacks; diminishing its capacity to generate funding; and restoring legitimate governance and security in Iraq will all have the effect of degrading ISIL's capacity.

In the longer term, the defeat of ISIL will come when it no longer has a safe haven from which to operate, when it no longer poses an existential threat to Iraq and other states in the region, and when the coalition effectively counters its global reach in spreading its message and ideology of hate, thus preventing it from regenerating over time. With regard to fully eradicating, annihilating or destroying all remnants of ISIL, like other terrorist groups before it, there will likely be some residue of the organization for a long time to come. We do not refer to disabling or containing ISIL.

RESPONSES OF GEN. JOHN R. ALLEN TO QUESTIONS
SUBMITTED BY SENATOR MARCO RUBIO

Question. How many countries is ISIL currently present in? Would you agree that we need an AUMF that is not specific to just Iraq and Syria?

Answer. ISIL's strongholds are in Iraq and Syria; however, ISIL seeks to extend its reach, and that is something we are monitoring closely.

The administration's proposed AUMF does not include a geographic limitation, as we believe it would be a mistake to advertise to ISIL that there are safe havens for them outside of Iraq and Syria by limiting the proposed AUMF to specific countries.

Question. Will ISIL be defeated by 2018?

Answer. Our Counter-ISIL strategy aims to degrade ISIL in Iraq and Syria over the course of a multiyear timeframe, leading to its eventual defeat. This will be a long-term effort, and it would be premature at this point to assign a completion date to it.

Degrading ISIL involves suppressing its ability to conduct large-scale operations. In the immediate to medium term, conducting military operations to halt and reverse ISIL territorial expansion; reducing its capability to resource, plan and execute offensive and/or terrorist attacks; diminishing its capacity to generate funding; and restoring legitimate governance and security in Iraq will all have the effect of degrading ISIL's capacity.

The defeat of ISIL will come in the longer term, when it no longer has a safe haven from which to operate, when it no longer poses an existential threat to Iraq and other states in the region, and when the coalition effectively counters its global reach in spreading its message and ideology of hate, thus preventing it from regenerating over time. Like the process of degrading ISIL, defeating ISIL must also take place over a multiyear timeframe.

Question. What is your understanding of the definition of "enduring offensive ground combat operations" in the White House's proposed AUMF?

Answer. As the President noted in his letter transmitting the proposed AUMF to the Congress, the proposal would not authorize long-term, large-scale ground combat operations like those our Nation conducted in Iraq and Afghanistan. As I testified before this committee in December, such operations will be the responsibility of local forces because that is what our local partners and allies want, that is what is best for preserving our international coalition, and most importantly, that is in the best interest of the United States.

The President has been clear, however, that there always may be exigent or unforeseen circumstances in which small numbers of U.S. forces may need to engage in limited or short duration ground combat operations, for example, to protect and defend U.S. personnel or citizens. The proposed AUMF would therefore provide the flexibility to conduct ground combat operations in other, more limited circumstances, such as rescue operations involving U.S. or coalition personnel or the use of special operations forces to take military action against ISIL leadership. The proposal would also authorize the use of U.S. forces in situations where ground combat operations are not expected or intended, such as intelligence collection and sharing, missions to enable kinetic strikes, or the provision of operational planning and other forms of advice and assistance to partner forces.

As the ground combat limitation is focused on major operations—long-term, large-scale—the proposal would provide the authority and the flexibility required to perform the mission.

Question. Why would we not authorize the President to simply achieve a mission rather than telling him to do so in a certain time period and only using certain means?

Answer. The President's goal is to secure the passage of a bipartisan, limited, ISIL-specific AUMF that will provide a clear signal to the American people, to our allies, and to our enemies that the United States stands united behind the effort to degrade and ultimately defeat ISIL. The President has developed and transmitted to the Congress an AUMF that reflects bipartisan input and contains reasonable limitations and that provides the flexibility he needs to successfully pursue the armed conflict against ISIL.

Although the proposed AUMF would not authorize long-term, large-scale ground combat operations like those our Nation conducted in Iraq and Afghanistan, it would provide the flexibility to conduct ground combat operations in other, more limited circumstances, such as rescue operations involving U.S. or coalition personnel or special operations forces to take military action against ISIL leadership. The proposal would also authorize the use of U.S. forces in situations where ground combat operations are not expected or intended, such as intelligence collection and sharing, missions to enable kinetic strikes, or the provision of operational planning and other forms of advice and assistance to partner forces.

In addition, although the confrontation with ISIL will not be over quickly, the President believes that 3 years is an appropriate period of time in order to allow the next President, the Congress, and the American people to assess the progress we have made against ISIL and review these authorities again.

We therefore believe that the proposed AUMF provides the authority and the flexibility required to perform the mission.

Question. You commanded U.S. forces in Afghanistan and Iraq. Put yourself in your former positions as a commander. Do you believe that it makes sense for politicians to prematurely tell our military how they need to win a military conflict?

Answer. Civilian control over the military is a bedrock principle of the Constitution. We are strongest as a nation when the administration and Congress work together on issues as serious as the use of military force.

The President proposed AUMF contains reasonable limitations and that would provide him with the flexibility to direct our military in successfully pursuing the armed conflict against ISIL.

Over the past several weeks, we have engaged in substantial consultations with Congress regarding the AUMF. We look forward to continuing to work with the Congress on this issue.

Question. How many countries was ISIL present in last August when coalition operations began?

Answer. From the evidence we have seen, ISIL had an operational presence in Iraq, Syria, and Lebanon in August 2014. The international community and the Global Coalition continue to diminish ISIL's capacity to generate revenues and fund its operations, cut off the flow of foreign terrorist fighters transiting to Iraq and Syria, and expose its empty and destructive ideology.

In fact, since September 2014, coalition efforts have forced ISIL to change its tactics and it is suffering significant losses, reducing its morale and challenging its ongoing propaganda campaigns.

Question. Why has ISIL continued to expand its reach despite our military operations?

Answer. While military operations against ISIL have succeeded in significantly reducing the area of ISIL-held territory in Iraq, a number of terrorist groups in other part of Muslim-majority countries have chosen to affiliate themselves with ISIL. These new ISIL affiliates do not appear to be established by an influx of ISIL militants, but rather, by a rebranding of already existing violent extremist organizations as ISIL franchises. We are monitoring the situation carefully to ascertain the extent to which these new affiliates benefit materially and doctrinally from their association with ISIL.

The strategy to combat these ISIL-related groups outside of Iraq and Syria leverages the broad capabilities of the United States, coalition members, and international partners across the globe. The strategy rests on the foundation of degrading and then destroying the self-proclaimed "Islamic State." Coalition efforts in Iraq and Syria—such as helping Iraqi security forces reclaim territory held by ISIL, suppressing ISIL's ability to conduct large-scale operations, degrading its command, control and logistics capabilities, and building the political foundations for long-term security—will inhibit the group's capability to operate globally and expand.

Beyond Iraq and Syria, the international community and the global coalition continue to diminish ISIL's capacity to generate revenues and fund its operations, cut off the flow of foreign terrorist fighters transiting to, and from, Iraq and Syria, and expose its empty and destructive ideology. Starving any new ISIL-related groups of funds and manpower reduces any of the groups' opportunity to expand or conduct attacks against our international partners. Following meetings with coalition members which Secretary Kerry chaired in December and January , coalition working groups are now coordinating combined efforts to address ISIL's finances, foreign fighter draw, and messaging and thereby diminish ISIL's global potential.

As these ISIL-related groups have emerged, the United States has also been working closely with our partners to reduce the safe havens that many of these groups exploit, build effective governance and security, strengthen the capacity of our partners to deal with these threats internally, enhance economic opportunity, and disrupt any plots.

Question. What is the strategy and timetable for an Iraqi security forces offensive to recapture Mosul and other areas still held by ISIL?

Answer. Any offensive will not begin until the Iraqis have determined they are ready. We are focused on getting the Iraqi security forces (ISF) adequately trained and equipped and the plan synchronized. This training is a critical component to our ultimate success because it is what will help generate durable security that exists beyond our direct military engagements.

Any action on Mosul or other areas needs to be methodical, coordinated, and planned properly. We are working with the Government of Iraq on isolating Mosul by cutting ISIL's lines of communication, eroding its forces through the air campaign, building combat power through the Building Partner Capacity sites, and helping with planning and synchronizing all of these elements to set the conditions for an offensive.

I would refer you to the Department of Defense and the Government of Iraq for any future operational planning, but as we have said, any operation on Mosul would be Iraqi-led and we are committed to working with the Iraqi security forces to degrade and defeat ISIL.

The timing of a campaign to liberate Mosul in relation to other important population centers and infrastructure in Iraq will depend on the political and military conditions on the ground and require strategic flexibility. Regardless of timing, our shared goal is clear: the defeat of ISIL and ensuring that ISIL can no longer pose a threat to the people of Iraq and to other countries in the region.

Question. What is the U.S. strategy to combat the rise of ISIS in other countries outside of Iraq and Syria?

Answer. The strategy to combat ISIL and related groups outside of Iraq and Syria rests on the coalition efforts within Iraq and Syria. In Iraq, the coalition is helping Iraqi security forces reclaim territory held by ISIL, suppressing ISIL's ability to conduct large-scale operations, degrading its command, control, and logistics capabilities, and building the political foundations for long-term security. In Syria, more than 1,200 coalition airstrikes against ISIL targets have destroyed ISIL vehicles and buildings, have degraded its economic infrastructure, and have defended local forces contesting ISIL advances, such as in Kobani. Our efforts in Syria will deny ISIL safe haven while creating the conditions for a stable inclusive Syria that fulfills Syrian's aspirations for freedom and dignity. Our counter-ISIL strategy in both countries will inhibit the group's capability to operate globally and expand. In fact, since September 2014, coalition efforts have forced ISIL to change its tactics and it is suffering significant losses, reducing its morale, and challenging its ongoing propaganda campaigns.

Beyond Iraq and Syria, the international community and the global coalition continue to diminish ISIL's capacity to generate revenues and fund its operations, cut off the flow of foreign terrorist fighters transiting to, and from, Iraq and Syria, and expose its empty and destructive ideology.

Starving any new ISIL-related groups of funds and manpower mitigates the risk of attacks against our international partners. Over the past 6 months, the international community has been increasing its efforts to expose the true nature of ISIL to reduce its draw to foreign fighters and other extremist groups. Similarly, international organizations and local communities across the globe are also increasingly working to minimize the influence of this hateful rhetoric and insulate potentially vulnerable sectors of populations. Following meetings with coalition members which Secretary Kerry chaired in December and January, coalition working groups are now coordinating combined efforts to address ISIL's finances, foreign fighter draw, and messaging and thereby diminish ISIL's global potential.

As these ISIL-related groups have emerged, the United State has also been working closely with our partners to reduce the safe havens that many of these groups exploit, build effective governance and security, strengthen the capacity of our partners to deal with these threats internally, enhance economic opportunity, and disrupt any plots. The United States continues to emphasize the importance of a multi-faceted, multinational approach to addressing ISIL and other extremist groups.

Question. The administration has built its strategy against ISIL around the notion that local partners will be trained and equipped to do much of the fighting, yet many key partners continue to complain about the level of support and communication they receive from the U.S. Government. The Kurds continue to request additional weapons, Sunni tribes in Iraq and Syria complain that their communities have endured massacres at the hands of ISIL, yet their requests for assistance have not been responded to. Meanwhile, the Syrian opposition has faced significant setbacks on the battlefield and they have raised fundamental concerns about U.S. strategy in Syria.

♦How do you address these criticisms?

Answer. Our military support to our local partners in Iraq remains steadfast and suggestions to the contrary do not reflect what we have witnessed so far. As the President has stressed, the campaign to degrade and defeat ISIL will take time, however, we have been able to reverse ISIL's momentum and the Iraqis continue to retake territory.

Through more than 2,700 coordinated coalition airstrikes in support of our partners on the ground, we have degraded ISIL's leadership, logistical, and operational capabilities, and are denying sanctuary in Iraq from which it can plan and execute attacks. Over 1,800 American and international troops, from a dozen countries, are training Iraqi and Kurdish security forces at Building Partner Capacity (BPC) sites around the country. Prime Minister Abadi has stated his appreciation for U.S. and coalition assistance on a number of occasions.

Regarding U.S. assistance to the Kurds in Iraq, U.S. military personnel are providing support for ISF and peshmerga on planning ground operations, intelligence-sharing, integrating air support into their operations, logistics planning, command and control, and communications. We established a Joint Operations Center in Erbil that has facilitated unprecedented cooperation between the KRG, Iraqi Government, and U.S. forces, and sent U.S. advise-and-assist teams to partner with peshmerga for operational planning. The Iraq Train and Equip Fund (ITEF) will provide an estimated $350 million to train and equip Kurdish brigades. To date, the coalition has provided the Kurds nearly 50 million rounds of light and heavy ammunition; 24,000 hand grenades; 47,000 mortar rounds; 50,000 RPG cartridges; and 18,000 rifles. This is in addition to the more than 300 tons of arms and ammunition that the Government of Iraq itself provided and delivered to the Kurds. We have also provided 25 MRAPs to our Kurdish partners. Hundreds of air strikes have supported the Kurds, striking ISIL elements in Mosul, near Sinjar Mountain, and other areas of northern Iraq providing relief to Kurdish forces and strategic opportunities to fight back against ISIL.

ITEF also allocates funding for the equipping of GOI-approved Sunni tribal fighters. On Sunni communities specifically, through our airstrikes and advise-and-assist teams, we have helped to protect key terrain and regain ground at Mosul Dam and around Haditha Dam in Anbar province. We also helped break the siege of Dhuluyia with airstrikes in support of Iraqi security forces and Sunni tribes when ISIL had that town surrounded. While we recognize that a variety of logistical challenges remain, we are working with the Government of Iraq to overcome these.

Question. Given the central focus of our strategy on empowering local allies to combat ISIL, why have we been so slow to provide the Jordanians, Kurds, and others with requested assistance?

Answer. Jordan has been a critical partner to the United States for many years. In support of our renewed Memorandum of Understanding signed by Secretary Kerry and Foreign Minister Judeh on February 3, we recently released $300 million in FY15 Foreign Military Financing several months earlier than it is generally released for other FMF recipient countries. We expect to provide additional FY15 FMF to Jordan once the post-appropriation allocations are finalized. And we are expediting delivery of a wide variety of military equipment.

The U.S. military is also directly enabling Jordanian counter-ISIL air strikes by providing targets, intelligence, fuel and training on refueling operations, dropping precision guided munitions, and night operations. This supplements long-standing military-to-military support and cooperation, such as U.S. Special Operations Forces training of their Jordanian counterparts and U.S. Army and Marine individual, collective, and unit training focused on border security techniques, tactics, and procedures for five Jordanian brigade- and battalion-sized formations.

Jordan's contributions to the global coalition against ISIL underline the continued importance of our bilateral partnership; the Departments of State and Defense have mobilized to support these Jordanian operations. Jordan has increased its anti-ISIL military operations following the appalling murder of its pilot, Captain Moaz al-Kasasbeh, and we have increased our efforts to coordinate with the JAF to further specify and prioritize its requirements. We have taken the following steps to support Jordan:

- To ensure Jordan can continue its airstrikes, we have expedited delivery of more than 200 bombs for its F–16s months early, with hundreds more on the way.
- To help Jordan prepare for ground combat contingencies, on February 7, the United States delivered to Jordan 20,000 rifles, 6,746 machine guns, and over 1 million rounds of small arms ammunition. One-thousand night vision devices are being drawn from U.S. military stocks and will be delivered to Jordan soon.
- We have notified Congress of our intent to provide eight Blackhawk helicopters to Jordan though a 2-year, no-cost lease as we pursue options to provide a larger, permanent capability in the long-term.

KURDISH ASSISTANCE

We have enormous respect for the courage the Kurds have shown and the fight they have taken to ISIL in Iraq and Syria. In coordination with the Government of Iraq, the United States and the coalition have been very supportive of Iraqi Kurdish forces, and coalition airstrikes were key to defeating an ISIL attempt to take the predominantly Kurdish city of Kobane in Syria.

- In Iraq, we have organized a coalition effort that to date has provided nearly 50 million rounds of light and heavy ammunition; 24,000 hand grenades; 47,000 mortar rounds; 50,000 RPG cartridges; and 18,000 rifles. Thousands more rounds of ammunition and weapons have been identified for donation and are being prepared for delivery. This is in addition to the more than 300 tons of arms and ammunition that the Government of Iraq itself provided and delivered to the Kurds. We have also provided 25 MRAPs to our Kurdish partners.
- Additionally, we will provide an estimated $350 million of ITEF to train and equip Kurdish brigades. While no equipment has yet been delivered under ITEF, these units will receive the same weapons, vehicles, and equipment as the Iraq Army forces: small arms, mortars, HMMWVs, cargo trucks, trailers, radios. Training began in Erbil in December.
- Hundreds of air strikes have supported peshmerga forces, striking ISIL elements in Mosul, near Sinjar Mountain, and other areas of northern Iraq providing relief to Kurdish forces and strategic opportunities to fight back against ISIL.
- We established a Joint Operations Center in Erbil that has facilitated unprecedented cooperation between the KRG, Iraqi Government, and U.S. forces, and sent U.S. and coalition advise-and-assist special forces teams to partner with peshmerga forces for operational planning.
- We will continue to evaluate the needs of all of Iraq's security forces, including the Kurdish security forces, to ensure that they have the necessary weapons to defeat ISIL.
- In Syria, we provided critical assistance to the Kurdish and Free Syrian Army forces defending the city of Kobane from ISIL advances. We launched more than 700 airstrikes to target ISIL positions and equipment, enabling the Kurdish ground forces to enhance the town's defenses, to prevent ISIL from attacking, and to extend security in the areas around Kobane. In addition, the United States bolstered Kobane's defenders by air with supplies provided by Kurdistan Regional Government authorities in Iraq, in addition to facilitating the entry of Iraqi peshmerga forces into northern Syria to assist those defending Kobane.
- Following ISIL's defeat in Kobane, military airstrikes in the vicinity of Kobane continue to support the efforts of Kurdish and Free Syrian Army forces to push ISIL from the surrounding areas.

Question. A key component of our strategy is the train-and-equip effort related to Syria. What pledges is the administration making to those Syrian rebel forces that agree to participate in coalition training programs regarding air support and ultimate plans to fight the Assad regime?

Answer. Our effort to equip appropriately vetted Syrian opposition elements has specific objectives: to defend the Syrian people from attacks by ISIL and secure territory controlled by the Syrian opposition; to protect the United States, its friends and allies, and the Syrian people from the threats posed by terrorists in Syria; and to promote the conditions for a negotiated settlement to end the conflict in Syria. We are committed to the success of the personnel we will train. The nature and extent of the support the United States is prepared to provide to those forces are critically important and under active consideration.

Question. Does the AUMF, as currently drafted, allow U.S. forces to provide defensive assistance to trained Syrian opposition forces from all of the threats they face, including from the Assad regime?

Answer. The President has been clear that he wants to work with Congress on a bipartisan, ISIL-specific AUMF. That is the immediate focus. Consistent with that focus, the administration's proposed AUMF would provide authority for the military mission we are currently undertaking in Iraq and Syria against ISIL.

We believe that Assad has lost the legitimacy to govern, but we are not asking for authority to use force against the Assad regime.

The nature and extent of the support the United States is prepared to provide to the Syrian forces we train is critically important and under active consideration. We plan to provide a level of support that is sufficient to support the objectives of the T&E program.

Question. What is Iran's level of control over the Shiite militias that have been mobilized to defend Baghdad and other areas in southern Iraq?

Answer. The threat of ISIL in Iraq has provided Iran with the opportunity for unprecedented cooperation with the Government of Iraq. However, Iranian influence in Iraq is not new. Iran has been a major player there since 2003.

Shia volunteers are an element of the fighting force against ISIL inside Iraq. Many are militia forces that formed last summer as a result of Grand Ayatollah Sistani's call for volunteers when Baghdad and other major cities were under imminent threat. Iran wields varying degrees of influence over these many different Iraqi Shiite militias, from high to negligible.

Where influence exists, it may not extend throughout the entire command structure of a militia making some members nonresponsive to Iranian direction.

Question. How would you characterize the role that Iran is currently playing in the fight against ISIL in Iraq? What level of coordination is there between coalition forces and Iran?

Answer. Iran is providing significant military support to the Iraqi security forces, Iraqi Shia volunteers and militias, and Kurdish forces in the form of weapons, combat advisors, training, intelligence, artillery support, and a handful of airstrikes. Iran is seeking to leverage and publicly highlight its military support in the counter-ISIL campaign for additional influence in Iraq.

Iran has channeled most of its support to Iraqi Shia groups under the Popular Mobilization Committee (PMC), upon which the Iraqi Government has relied heavily in recent counter-ISIL operations. The PMC is comprised of many untrained Iraqi volunteers, to include some Sunni tribes, as well as more hard-line sectarian militias heavily influenced by Iran. The Government of Iraq is seeking to differentiate between Iranian proxy groups and Iraqi volunteers in an effort to limit Iran's influence and gain better control over the security forces.

We recognize that Iraq and Iran share a long physical border, and that Iraq and Iran will have a relationship. And it is also clear that ISIL is a threat to the entire region, including Iran, and we understand that Iran is pursuing its own actions against ISIL in Iraq. But to adequately address the threat posed by ISIL and ensure long-term stability in Iraq, ISIL can only be defeated by an integrated and capable Iraqi security force backed by a unified Iraq.

Question. What is Iran's current relationship toward the Assad regime in Syria and to ISIL forces in Syria?

Answer. Iran has been a critical support line to the Assad regime, providing not only funds and weapons, but also strategic guidance, technical assistance, and training. This support has enabled the regime to continue its repression and slaughter of tens of thousands of Syrians, which has also fostered the emergence and expansion of extremist groups such as ISIL. Many analysts assess that Iran's assistance has been crucial to helping the Assad regime survive to date.

We know that Iran is supplying arms to the Syrian regime in violation of the U.N. Security Council prohibition against Iran selling or transferring arms and related materials, including through flights over Iraqi territory.

This issue has been raised with Iraqi officials by Secretary Kerry and other senior U.S. officials, emphasizing the connection between the flow of weapons and the escalation of extremist violence in the region, particularly in Syria. We have urged that Iraq either deny overflight requests for Iranian aircraft going to Syria, or require such flight to land in Iraq for credible inspections, consistent with its international legal obligations.

Question. ISIS is now a threat to all Syrians and Iraqis regardless of their religious faith, but the smallest religious communities, including Catholics, Syriac Christians, Protestants, Yazidis, and Sabean Mandaeans, face an existential threat. ISIS has committed countless acts of crimes against humanity, including murder through beheadings, enslavement of women and children, and torture.

◆ How can the United States and its coalition partners protect the smallest communities from complete eradication in Syria, Iraq, or anywhere else ISIS is a threat? How can the United States best work with our partners to help ensure the region's religious diversity and the protection of freedom of religion or belief?

Answer. The United States has long been concerned about the safety and rights of members of Iraq's and Syria's vulnerable populations, including members of religious and ethnic minorities. Protecting these communities and others in the face of the existential threat from ISIL is one of the priorities of our counter-ISIL strategy and of the 62-nation international counter-ISIL coalition, as well a part of our regular diplomatic engagement.

The United States and certain coalition partners have conducted a campaign of coordinated airstrikes against ISIL, and the coalition also has undertaken military assistance, diplomatic engagement, and intelligence and messaging coordination to defeat, degrade, and delegitimize ISIL. Through these actions, we have dealt ISIL strategic blows, halting its advances and preventing atrocities, beginning with the airstrikes President Obama announced August 7, 2014, to help the Yezidis stranded on Mt. Sinjar, and followed by airstrikes and the delivery of relief supplies to the Shia Turkmen in Amerli.

The United States has regular and ongoing contact with leaders of minority religious groups in the United States and throughout the Middle East region to discuss their well-being and needs. The Office of International Religious Freedom in the Bureau of Democracy, Human Rights and Labor has been especially helpful in this outreach. Our contacts include Christian leaders, Yezidi activists, civil society and clergy members, minority diaspora, and advocacy groups. In Iraq, the U.S. Embassy in Baghdad and consulate general in Erbil are in daily contact with the Iraqi Government, the Kurdistan Regional Government, the U.N., and other humanitarian aid organizations in Iraq to ensure they do their utmost to reach and assist displaced Iraqis—including minorities.

It is very difficult to reach areas of Syria and Iraq that are under the control of ISIL. Despite these challenges, the United States continues to work closely with humanitarian organizations to find ways to try to provide life-saving aid to those who need it. The U.N., which is overseeing the massive international effort to aid those fleeing areas in, or at risk of, conflict, is also in regular contact with minority groups and their leaders. Representatives of these communities have expressed the importance of not only food, shelter, and clean water, but of educational opportunities for children, job opportunities for young people, and medical services for displaced communities to avoid the need to relocate to a third country while ISIL is being defeated. The United States remains the single largest donor to the humanitarian response for Syria, contributing more than $3 billion in life-saving humanitarian aid to Syrian IDPs and refugees in the region since the crisis began. The United States also continues to be a primary donor to displaced Iraqis, contributing over $219 million since fiscal year 2014.

In Iraq, we are working with the Government of Iraq, the U.N., and our coalition partners to create the conditions for the displaced to return to their homes as soon as possible, and we will continue to press the Government of Iraq and support its efforts to ensure that minority communities are able to return to their homes in peace. This includes support for Prime Minister Abadi's efforts to devolve power from the federal government to provincial and local authorities as an important mechanism for protecting the rights of all Iraqis and to preserve the unity and long-term stability of Iraq. We are also encouraging the establishment of an Iraqi National Guard, which would provide a stable mechanism for local communities, including minority communities, to take more responsibility for their own protection while receiving the resources and training needed to do so. In Syria, the United States will continue to work toward a negotiated political solution that produces a stable, inclusive Syria for people of all ethnic and religious identities, a Syria free from the tyranny of the Assad regime and the terror of ISIL.

Question. ISIL's extremist ideology disallows any religious diversity or religious freedom. Increasingly, minority communities, especially in Iraq, report they will not attempt to return after years of targeting because they simply do not trust the government or their neighbors.

◆ How are issues of religious freedom, human rights, interfaith dialogue, or respect for diversity and pluralism being made part of the strategy to fight against ISIS?

Answer. We will not degrade and defeat ISIL through military effort alone. An important component of our work requires promotion of an open and inclusive society, which can win out against its repressive and divisive ideology. This demands a society that respects the rights to all citizens regardless of religious identity or other distinction, and that also respects diversity, including members of religious and ethnic minorities, women, and those voicing different political views.

In Iraq, Prime Minister Abadi has made important strides to reduce sectarian tensions and promote inclusivity including, for example, the proposed National Guard law, his statements regarding a ''zero tolerance'' policy for human rights violations, and his efforts to incorporate militias into existing security structures, as well as his Executive order to adhere to Iraqi law regarding the time detainees may be held in custody—a key concern of the Sunnis. We will support him in these efforts and urge him to implement them.

We are working to promote and establish an inclusive, rights-respecting governance system in Iraq, especially in regards to the security forces, to prevent marginalization and minimize sectarian hostilities. We seek the same thing in Syria through a negotiated political solution that fulfills Syrians' aspirations for freedom and dignity. These efforts include focusing on respect for human rights in our engagements with military and civilian leaders and incorporating law of armed conflict training in our plans to train and equip both Iraqi security forces and vetted elements of the Syrian opposition.

We are supporting the Iraqi Government and civil society to reconstitute those areas that have been liberated from ISIL control with those communities who were forced to flee, rebuilding toward tolerance and peaceful coexistence. Our projects engage and support members of religious and ethnic minorities in Iraq, aiming to increase community representation and participation by minorities, bolster advocacy on their behalf, and promote the peaceful rebuilding of Iraqi communities. In Syria we are supporting interim governance structures, as well as local and provincial councils, civil society organizations, and local security actors, setting a course toward a peaceful, democratic, inclusive future and helping establish the conditions for a political solution to this conflict. We also support programs to empower religious and ethnic minorities and promote tolerance and reconciliation to counter rising sectarian tensions, among others; for instance, we have hosted multiple Syrian interfaith conferences and activities both in the United States and in the region that featured prominent Syrian clergy of all backgrounds with large followings. Additionally, the Department of State played a key role in the White House-hosted summit on Countering Violent Extremism in February 2015, which Syrian and Iraqi civil society and clergy representatives attended and which has resulted in renewed attention to role of governance and human rights in the fight against violent extremism.

www.ingramcontent.com/pod-product-compliance
Lightning Source LLC
Chambersburg PA
CBHW081757280526
45789CB00008B/2895